Discovering London
in the 21ˢᵗ Century

HIROMICHI NISHINO

RYUTSU KEIZAI UNIVERSITY PRESS

MAP OF LONDON

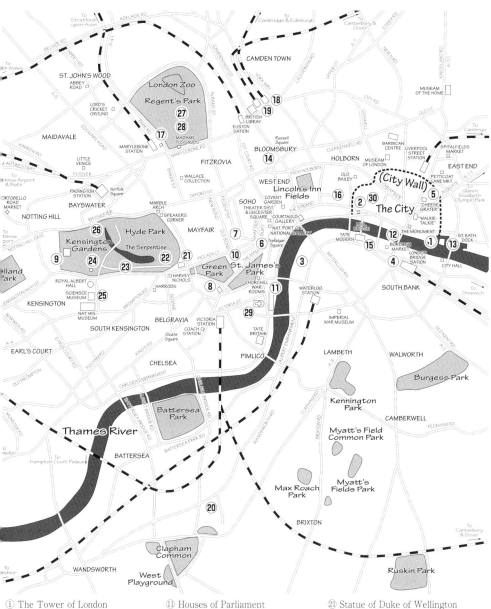

① The Tower of London
② St Paul's Cathedral
③ London Eye
④ The Shard
⑤ The Gherkin
⑥ Piccadilly Circus
⑦ Regent Street
⑧ Buckingham Palace
⑨ Kensington Palace
⑩ St James's Palace

⑪ Houses of Parliament
⑫ London Bridge
⑬ Tower Bridge
⑭ British Museum
⑮ Shakespeare's Globe
⑯ Dr Johnson's House
⑰ The Sherlock Holmes Museum
⑱ King's Cross Station
⑲ St Pancras International Station
⑳ Soseki's boarding house

㉑ Statue of Duke of Wellington
㉒ Rose Garden
㉓ Rotten Row
㉔ Albert Memorial
㉕ Victoria & Albert Museum
㉖ Peter Pan Statue
㉗ Triton and Dryads Fountain
㉘ The Japanese Garden Island
㉙ Westminster Abbey
㉚ Church of St Mary-Le-Bow

Regent Street just after the coronation of Charles III

CONTENTS

Kensington Palace

Introduction

A Brief History of the British Isles

The British Isles were connected to continental Europe more than 10,000 years ago, but gradually, the current topography was formed after a long time. From about 5,000 BC, the Iberians who originated in North Africa and settled in southern Europe migrated to England and practiced cattle raising and farming. Later, from Europe, the Beakers invaded, leaving stone circles such as Stonehenge in Salisbury. The Beakers also pastured, but armed themselves with bows and arrows to prepare for foreign enemies. Later, the Celts came from the center of continental Europe, used iron (and bronze) tools and weapons instead of conventional stone and bronze ones, and built many hillforts, the earliest forms of castles at that time, on hills (around 700-500 BC). In 55-54 BC, Consul Julius Caesar, a Roman led a fleet to invade Britain, and in 43 AD the Roman troops advanced in earnest and finally conquered all of England. The Roman army built many Roman forts, full-scale stone military installations in every place, and many Romanized cities appeared.

Many Roman roads were built and Hadrian's Wall was built on the border with Scotland in 128 AD. Pursued by Germanic tribes invading from northwestern Europe, the Romans withdrew completely from England in 410. Britain, which had been governed by the Romans, was now oppressed by the Jutes, Angles, and Saxons, who by the 6th century had driven the indigenous Celts to Wales, Scotland, and other backwaters and settled in England. They built fortified settlements called Burgs (Saxon Forts) in various places.

Areas dominated by the Angles were called Angles-land, which eventually became known as England. In the 8th century, Viking invasions began from the Scandinavian Peninsula, and in 1016 King Canute of Denmark became King of England. After that, the English king became Anglo-Saxon again, but in 1066, when King Edward the Confessor died, England was immediately conquered by William, Duke of Normandy, France, and William became King William I of England. Thereafter, in England, the ruling class was Norman French, the common people were Germanic, and French was spoken in castles and Anglo-Saxon in castle towns. Anglo-Saxon culture eventually merged with French culture, and so did the language, becoming English.

William I (William the Conqueror) built solid castles in various places and ruled over all of England with a network of castles. During the reign of King John (reigned 1199-1216), the French territories inherited from the previous kings were lost, and the royal power was restricted in domestic affairs, triggering the beginning of parliamentary politics.

Wales has a harsh climate and many steep mountains. The Welsh lived in different tribes in each region, and there was no unified dynasty. Few lived in towns and villages, kept livestock and built shabby huts woven from twigs. Battles between the tribes were constantly repeated, and when the enemy attacked, the clans packed up and fled to the forests to fight back with guerrilla warfare. There was no armor, and weapons were large bows, swords, throwing spears, etc., and it is said that they fought barefoot even in the harsh winter.

Originally, most of the Welsh were the indigenous Celts of England, who once lived in the plains and fertile regions of England, but were driven to Wales by the invasions of the Romans, Anglo-Saxons, and Vikings.

During the Seven Anglo-Saxon Kingdoms (Northumbria, Mercia, East Anglia, Essex, Sussex, Wessex, and Kent), Offa, King of Mercia (756-96) built a great earthen barrier on the border between England and Wales, called the "Offa's Dyke" to cut off relations with the Welsh. William the Conqueror, after the conquest of England, also placed the Earl of Chester and the Earl of Shrewsbury on the border to monitor Wales. However, the border lords later invaded Wales and seized territory without the king's permission to expand their holdings. This is why early Norman noble castles and towns were established in the south and central Wales.

During the reign of Edward I (r. 1272-1307), the king completely conquered Wales and made an expedition to Scotland. During this period, fortified cities were formed in various places, and castles, cathedrals, city gates, city walls were constructed. Edward III (r. 1327-77) sought the former French territories, which led to the Hundred Years' War between England and France (1337-1453). Then, due to the failure of the Anglo-French War, the succession to the throne problem occurred in

Ruins of Hadrian's Wall built by the Roman army

9

Queen Victoria

England, and the House of Lancaster (Red Rose) and York (White Rose) fought each other, resulting in the so-called Wars of the Roses (1455-85). Eventually, Henry VII of the Red Rose (r. 1485-1509) won and the Tudor dynasty began. The next king, Henry VIII (r. 1509-47) carried out setting up his own Church of England (breaking away from the Catholic Church) due to his personal divorce problems, and succeeded in modernizing England. The king built many military fortifications along the coastline in preparation for the attack from France and Spain.

After Queen Mary the Catholic, England became Protestant again when her sister Elizabeth was Queen (r. 1558-1603), and the nation prospered even more than in the time of her father, Henry VIII, and the navy was strengthened. In 1588, English ships (sea dogs) defeated the Spanish Armada, which was praised as the strongest in Europe at the time, in the English Channel (Battle of Armada).

As overseas expansion was promoted, the East India Company (a semi-public, semi-private company) advanced to Japan via India, China, and Indonesia, and opened a trading house in Hirado, Japan. Textiles and *cha* (green tea) were imported to England, and *cha* became British tea. But later, Hirado was closed and replaced by Nagasaki due to the new policy of the Edo shogunate. It was also during this period that William Shakespeare (1564-1616), the world's greatest writer, was active. After Queen Elizabeth's death, James VI of Scotland became King James I of England, and his son Charles I came into conflict with Parliament, eventually leading to civil war, and the king was beheaded (1649). England became a temporary republic, but the monarchy was restored and Charles II ascended the throne (1660).

In the 18th century, a German prince, George of Hanover, the great-grandson of James I, became George I, and the Hanoverian dynasty started. All four kings went under the name of George. During this period, the Industrial Revolution occurred and the economy developed greatly. In the 19th century, England became the world's most powerful country, and Queen Victoria, who also served as Empress of India, became a symbol of the British Empire.

During the French Revolutionary Wars (1792-1802), the victory of the British fleet, led by Horatio Nelson (1758-1805) over the French fleet at the Battle of the Nile in 1798, resulted in Napoleon being isolated in Egypt and France ceding control of the Mediterranean to Britain. During the Napoleonic Wars (1803-15), Nelson defeated the combined Franco-Spanish fleet at the Battle of Trafalgar in 1805 to prevent the French invasion of the British mainland. Nelson is known for sending a message saying "England expects that every man will do his duty". Nelson was fatally wounded and died during the battle. The message must have meant that "Nelson will do his duty." In 1815, the Duke of Wellington (Arthur Wellesley, 1st Duke of Wellington, 1769-1852) defeated Napoleon's French army at Waterloo, Belgium, and Napoleon fled to Paris, where he finally surrendered

Horatio Nelson   Duke of Wellington

(Battle of Waterloo, Bataille de Waterloo).

England opened many colonies around the world and became the center of the British Empire. But in the 20th century, after two world wars, British colonies became independent, and now in the 21st century, the United Kingdom that has become the leader of the British Commonwealth in name only still does not lose its presence as the center of the world's leading developed countries, and advocates a new lifestyle such as how to live a 100-year-old life. The British are constantly disseminating information to the world. We could say that England is now a small but great country.

The Mall (Street connecting Buckingham Palace and Trafalgar Square)

1. A Brief History of London

The word "London" is said to have originated from the Celtic word "Llyn-dun", which meant "Riverside-hill". On the other hand, there is another theory that it is from "Londinos", which meant

Skyscrapers of the City

"Hill of the Strong Men" in the same Celtic language. Considering that the Romans named the place "Londinium", the latter may be possible. Ruled by the Romans, London had a population of over 30,000 in the 3rd century, becoming the fifth largest city in the Roman Empire. The city was surrounded by stone walls, forming a fortified city. When the Roman army withdrew, the Saxons entered London to live. They called London "Lundenwic", and "wic (wick)" meant "market town" or "port" in Anglo-Saxon (Old English). Their houses were mostly made of wood. St Paul's Cathedral, a Christian stronghold in London, was built of wood in the 7th century. In the 8th and 9th centuries, the Saxon city of London was attacked by the Vikings. *The Anglo-Saxon Chronicle* records the Battle of London Bridge. When England was conquered by William, Duke of Normandy in France in the 11th century, many Norman buildings were built in London, including the Tower of London, Westminster Abbey on the west side, and the stone reconstruction of St Paul's Cathedral, which had been made of wood. The symmetrical architecture made Londoners acutely aware of the arrival of a new era.

Already in the far west of the city, a new palace and abbey had been built by Edward the Confessor. The abbey was called West-minster as opposed to East-minster, St Paul's, in the east of London. The new abbey was a Norman building with two symmetrical spires. A Norman palace called Westminster Hall was also built right next to the new Westminster Abbey. Since William the Conqueror, successive kings of England have been crowned in the abbey. The White Tower of the Tower of London, the royal palace and fortress, was designed by Gundulph, Bishop of Rochester (1024-1108).

In the Middle Ages, London was damaged by great fires and plagues such as cholera. The Great Plague of 1665 killed 100,000 people (London's population at the time was 400,000) and the Great Fire of 1666 (which destroyed four-fifths of the city, burned 13,000 houses and affected 250,000 people) was a catastrophe. Thereafter, new buildings had to be made of brick or stone, but in practice, due to financial problems, the city was not allowed to be sufficiently remodeled.

Aristocrats who supported Henry Tudor in the Wars of the Roses, or Protestant courtiers and merchants who benefited from Henry VIII's Reformation, built residences in London with new estates. Former Catholic lands were confiscated and the king's vassals newly built country houses. During this time, a number of noble townhouses were built in the Strand area and near the Palace of Westminster. Henry VIII himself built a number of palaces in and around London, or confiscated estates from the archbishop and made them royal residences. During the reign of his daughter Elizabeth I, a plague broke out seriously in London, and the crowded theaters were closed.

St Paul's Cathedral

People fled from the dirty conditions of the big city to the countryside, and later James I ordered a ban on the construction of new buildings in London, especially around Westminster. Nevertheless, the courtiers' long stay in the London mansion expanded their power, eventually leading to civil war and the tragedy of the beheading of Charles I.

At the beginning of the 19th century, the population of London was 870,000, but by the 1880s, it numbered 5 million. The transportation network was improved, and an omnibus (horse-drawn carriage) appeared in the 1830s. London's first railway station was Euston in 1837. Stations such as Paddington, Victoria, St Pancras, and Liverpool Street were completed one after another. There is no central station in London called "London Station", and if you want to say so, Victoria Station would be the equivalent. By the 1860s, railroads were in practical use.

In the 20th century, London experienced two world wars, most notably the Luftwaffe (German Air Force) that attacked London in 1940, when many churches were damaged and about 80,000 people were either wounded or killed. In the 1960s and 70s, young people influenced by the Beatles roamed the streets and introduced new fashion and culture to the world.

The Blair government, which came into being in 1997, advocated a new policy of Modern Britain ahead of the millennium of the 21st century. And since the 21st century, there are a lot of modern buildings here and there in London. The British Museum was also extensively renovated to commemorate the millennium, and the British Library was moved to the outside to create the beautiful chalk space of the Great Court. Just like McDonald's once appeared, an American coffee shop called Starbucks appeared in London. The tolerant and flexible attitude makes the ancient capital London even richer. Linking St Paul's Cathedral to Tate Modern, the Millennium Bridge, a light aluminum footbridge that only humans can cross, was built over the River Thames in 2000.

Having 32 viewing capsules with a capacity of 25 people each, the London Eye, a 135-meter-high Ferris wheel, was built along the Thames. The time required for one rotation is 30 minutes. Originally opened in 1999 as part of the Millennium Project. It was a temporary attraction and was due to be removed in 2005, but it was so popular that the plan was changed and is now one of London's most iconic landmarks. After being operated by British Airways and others, it is now sponsored by Coca-Cola.

The Shard is a 310-meter-high, 95-story skyscraper office building located on the southwest side of London Bridge Station, completed in 2012. To be precise, the 2nd to 28th floors are offices, the 31st to 33rd floors are restaurants, the

London Eye

34th to 52nd floors are hotel rooms, the 53rd to 65th floors are apartments, the 68th to 72nd floors are observation facilities, and the 75th to 87th floors are the roof of the tower. The exterior walls of the tower, which was built in the image of a sailing ship

The Shard

The Gherkin

mast or a church spire, are covered with many pieces of glass and reflect various beautiful shades depending on the weather. "Shard" means a piece of broken pottery, rock, metal, or glass.

The Gherkin, officially called 30 St Mary Axe, is a 180-meter-high, all-glass, high-rise office building built in the financial district of the City of London. It is called the Gherkin because it resembles a cucumber. The upright building in the shape of a cone was designed by Norman Forster and completed in 2004.

It is still fresh in our memory that in 2012, the London Olympics were held. The opening ceremony was spectacular, with Shakespearean actor Sir Kenneth Branagh reading Shakespeare's *The Tempest*, actor Daniel Craig, who played the sixth James Bond, co-starring with Queen Elizabeth to perform "Her Majesty the Flying Queen", J.K. Rowling reading "Peter Pan", David Beckham appearing at the torch lighting, and Paul McCartney singing "Hey Jude" at the end. It was a flashy opening ceremony, and it seemed too hefty, but the London Olympics were an environmentally friendly event that set a model for the sustainable development of London after the Games. Sustainability was the key word of the

Piccadilly Circus   Regent Street

London Olympic Games. The main venue chosen was a soil-contaminated area where waste had been dumped and neglected for many years since the Industrial Revolution. Contaminated soil was purified, vast green spaces were developed, and the area was reborn.

London's biggest entertainment district is probably the area around Piccadilly Circus. Piccadilly Circus is a tourist spot crowded with many people day and night. The fountain with the statue of Eros in the center is famous as a meeting place. The West End's theater district is also nearby, so you can enjoy musicals at low prices. It is also connected to Regent Street, which is lined with shops, and the street has a beautiful six-story gently curved stone building on both sides, and there are many specialty stores. It was named after Prince Regent (later King George IV), who was called the most fashionable man in Europe at the beginning of the 19th century.

Dr. Johnson, a great man of literary London in the 18th century, once said, "When a man is tired of London, he is tired of life; for there is in London all life can afford." and it can be said that London continues to evolve further and fascinate people all over the world even now in the 21st century.

2. British Royal Family and Palaces

On the site of Buckingham Palace was originally Buckingham House which was built by the Duke of Buckingham in 1705. King George III bought the house and began living with Queen Charlotte, and the history of the palace began. It was here that King George III met with Dr. Johnson. Soon after his accession to the throne, King George IV ordered that Buckingham House be converted into an entirely new palace, which was completed in 1837. Queen Victoria first moved here from St James's Palace (and Kensington Palace) and this palace has since become the royal residence of successive kings and queens. King Charles III (1948-) was also born here. The square-shaped

Buckingham Palace

building with courtyard has more than 600 rooms. Tourists can enjoy the extremely picturesque view of King's Guards' marching in front of the palace, with their black bear-haired hats, red uniforms, and black trousers. The ceremony of changing the guard has

Kensington Palace (Entrance & Exit)

undoubtedly become the best tourist attraction in London. The Mall, a tree-lined avenue, stretches for one kilometer from the palace to Trafalgar Square. In front of the palace stands a 24.6-meter-tall marble statue of Queen Victoria, erected in 1911 by the Queen's grandson, King George V. This monument brings visual changes to the palace. Buckingham Palace is surrounded by parks on three sides, but the view of the palace from the pond in St James's Park is superb.

Kensington Palace is a Jacobean palace built during the reign of James I. In 1689, William III (r. 1689-1702) and Mary II (r. 1689-94) bought the house from the Earl of Nottingham and made it their new palace in London. Neither William III nor Mary II, who were suffering from chronic asthma at the time, liked

Kensington Palace and Gold Gates

Whitehall Palace in the heart of London, so the couple moved here from Hampton Court Palace. William III died here in 1702. Mary II's sister Queen Anne also died here in 1714. George I, the first of Hanover, and his son George II also lived in this palace. George III preferred Buckingham

House. The Duke of Kent made this palace his residence, and as a result, Queen Victoria was born in one of the rooms of Kensington Palace in 1819. Princess Victoria was raised in this palace, and it was here that she was woken up in her sleep in 1837 and informed that she had become Queen.

Main Entrance of St James's Palace

The gardens that have been open to the public since 1841 are called Kensington Gardens, and beyond Serpentine Pond (made by King George II in 1730) is another park called Hyde Park. The statue of Peter Pan is located on the Kensington Gardens side. In recent years, the current King Charles and the late Princess Diana are known to have lived together in Kensington Palace (1981-92). It remained Diana's residence after February 1996, when they officially divorced (Diana, the former Princess of Wales died in a car accident in Paris in August 1997). Currently, her son Prince William (the Prince of Wales) and his wife, Catherine, Princess of Wales, and their children Prince George (2013-), Princess Charlotte (2015-), and Prince Louis (2018-) live in the palace.

St James's Palace (Tudor red brick)

St James's Palace was built by Henry VIII in 1530 as a Tudor red brick palace. Queen Elizabeth I set up her court here, and the next James I also set up his court here. Charles I's sons, Charles II and James II were born here. James II's daughter, Queen Anne (r. 1702-14) and George IV were also born here. A grand celebration was held here in 1811 to celebrate George's appointment as regent. Charles I spent the night in this palace the day before his execution at Whitehall. At the time of the Glorious Revolution of 1689, William III is said to have effectively moved the royal palace from Whitehall to St James's Palace (and Kensington Palace). In 1698, it officially became the first royal palace, replacing the burned-down Whitehall Palace. George I, II, and III also made this palace their first royal residence. In 1809, the palace burned down, but by 1836 it had been completely rebuilt. The chapel and gatehouse remain intact as they were when Henry VIII built them. Queen Victoria's wedding took place here in 1840. Her grandson, King George V, also got married here. St James's Palace is still the Royal Court formally.

The Three Attractive Queens

If we take a look at the history of the successive kings and queens of Britain, we will see that the country reached a turning point in history when the Queen ruled. Especially during the reigns of Queen Elizabeth I in the 16ᵗʰ century, Queen Victoria in the 19ᵗʰ century, and Queen Elizabeth II in the 20ᵗʰ century, Britain made a huge leap forward as one of the world's leading nations, or Britain tried to remain a powerful nation in the world even though losing its colonies, economically weakened, and losing centripetal force it once had.

The 16ᵗʰ century was the beginning of the age of science. In 1510, Copernicus publicized the heliocentric theory: the sun is the center of the

Queen Elizabeth I

solar system and the earth is moving, not the sun. Galileo Galilei appreciated the theory. There is a famous anecdote that Galileo said, "The earth is still moving," after being convicted in 1633. The 16th century was also the dawn of the Age of Great Voyages. Many Europeans, especially Portuguese and Spanish, began to explore Africa and Asia. Christopher Columbus was the first European to land in America in 1492. Then England, France, and Holland began to explore North America. Sir Francis Drake (1543-96) was the first Englishman to sail around the world. That was the time when England was becoming more important in the world. At that time, England was ruled by Queen Elizabeth I (1533-1603) and in her reign, the playwright Shakespeare appeared. Moreover, England defeated the Spanish Armada in 1588. Queen Elizabeth, known as the Virgin Queen, became a symbol of modern Britain. And she fulfilled her duty.

During the Victorian Age (1837-1901), British Empire grew, and Britain became the richest and most powerful country in the world. It had the largest Empire, ruling one-fifth of the world's land and one-quarter of the people on the earth. During Victoria's reign, the British population grew from two million to six and a half million. Prince Albert, who was the husband of Queen Victoria, died in 1861, and the widowed Queen became a symbol of Britain. As a result of the Industrial Revolution, sciences developed dramatically. During her time, Britain was at war every day and night. As a result, Queen Victoria could rule many colonies around the world. If the head of the country had been King, would he have gained so many colonies? Could colonial rule have worked so well? By

Queen Victoria

bringing the idea of queen rule to the colonies, it may have had the effect of dispelling the image of holding down the country with powerful pressure. It's like a mother raising a child. Children usually listen to their mothers, but rebel against their fathers' opinions.

Queen Elizabeth II was born in London in 1926 to Albert, Duke of York (later George VI), and her mother, Elizabeth, daughter of the Earl of Strathmore of Scotland. She had loved dogs and horses since her childhood. In 1936, when her uncle, Edward VIII, abdicated to marry Wallis Simpson, an American, and her father ascended the throne as King George VI. Suddenly, Princess Elizabeth was first in line to the throne. During World War II, she served in the women's branch of the British Army, where she performed official duties such as ammunition management and driving military trucks. In the past, female royals were given titles in the military, but they were only honorary positions and did not actually serve. Despite the fact that she was confirmed to be the next Queen, Elizabeth received military training equivalent to other ordinary female soldiers. In 1947, she married Philip Mountbatten, who was born into the Greek and Danish royal families. They had three sons (Charles, Andrew, and Edward) and one girl (Anne). In 1952, at the age of 25, she became Queen Elizabeth II. At the same time, she became head of state of the British Commonwealth of Nations (the United Kingdom, Canada, Australia, New Zealand, South Africa, Pakistan, Ceylon, etc.). Her four children were not educated by the imperial court, but the Queen enrolled them in regular schools. It was truly for the first time for the children of the royal family. Queen Elizabeth's educational policies were inherited by Princess Diana. During her lifetime, the Queen visited more than 120 countries around the world to develop her royal diplomacy. In particular, she worked to restore Anglo-American relations. She constantly strived to bring the people closer to the royal family and to restore trust in the royal family after each scandal. Throughout her life, she was extremely busy. In 2022, she died of senility at Balmoral Castle, Scotland, at the age of 96. After a state funeral at Westminster Abbey, her body was buried in St George's Chapel in Windsor Castle. Three months after Queen Elizabeth's death, King Charles III sent a video message to the public, saying:

'To my darling Mama, as you begin your last great journey to join my dear late Papa, I want simply to say this: thank you. Thank you for your love and devotion to our family and to the family of nations you have served so diligently all these years. May "flights of angels sing thee to thy rest".'[1]

Queen Elizabeth II supported Britain well throughout the two world wars, losing its colonies and becoming only a small island nation on the edge of Europe. The public's criticism of the royal family increased, including the divorce of Prince Charles and Princess Diana, the subsequent accidental death of Princess Diana, the withdrawal of Prince Henry and his wife, Meghan from the royal family, the issue of Scottish independence, and also the withdrawal from the European Union becoming realistic. The Queen always tried overcoming such kind of crisis. It can be said that under Her Majesty, the Queen, aristocrats, politicians, business people, and the general public all worked together and did their duties. Her Majesty reigned when England was in great crisis as a nation. Usually, the King is a

Queen Elizabeth II

25

symbol and the country will be well organized. Sometimes, it is necessary for the King to show his strong leadership. Everyone works together under the rule of the King. In the case of a Queen, the vassals are willing to do their duties. The workplace will have more leeway and have a more open atmosphere. People are able to go as far as they can. Isn't that what it is? Basically, parent-child relationships often work better with mothers than with fathers.

Female names are used for ship names, and the sailors are united and the ship moves well. A strong leader will make everyone fear, impress, and pull. In the case of inexperienced and unreliable leaders, their subordinates think that they have to support their leaders and work hard voluntarily. There is no salvation in an organization with only subordinates who cannot do anything if the top management disappears. It is stronger as a group if everyone is individually strong because no matter who becomes the leader, the group is strong. It's better that way. However, there is always an attraction to a leader that everyone wants to support. Human charm is necessary. No doubt Queen Elizabeth II would have been such an attractive person, and above all, she was the Queen who truly embodied the words, Noblesse Oblige, cherished by the English aristocracy, which means the performance of the duties that come with high status. For me, the Queen even had the image of Joan of Arc (1412-31). Queen Elizabeth II was loved by everyone because she always carried out her job honestly.

Buckingham Palace in the afternoon

3. Palace of Westminster and Winston Churchill

The Palace of Westminster serves
as the Houses of Parliament, the political
center of the United Kingdom, and there
are the House of Lords and the House of
Commons. The West Monastery changed
to become Westminster. In the 11th
century, Edward the Confessor, who
built Westminster Abbey, built the

Palace of Westminster

residence (it is said that King Canute was the first to use it as a palace).
Formally, the first royal palace was constructed by William the Conqueror in the
11th century. The Palace is considered to be a key point politically and militarily
in west London (The key point on the east side is the Tower of London). Until the
16th century, it was used as the major royal residence. But after the Great Fire of
1529, Henry VIII moved to Palace of Whitehall the following year, and White
Hall Palace became the leading royal residence. After that, the Palace of
Westminster has continued as a place where the Model Parliament or
Representative Parliament has been held since 1295 during the reign of Edward I.

The Palace, which had survived for more than 300 years, was destroyed by
a fire in 1834. The present buildings (such as the clock tower Big Ben and
Victoria Tower) were built in the Neo-Gothic style in 1860-70, with the
exception of the Norman style Westminster Hall. In the reconstruction, it was
debated whether to adopt Gothic or neoclassical style, but the Neo-Gothic style
was adopted in response to the Gothic Revival movement at that time. It was

designed by Sir Charles Barry (1795-1860) and Augustus Pugin (1812-1852). The former preferred Italian classicism and the latter was a Gothic lover. Therefore, to be precise, the Palace of Westminster is a compromise between the two principles.

Horace Walpole (1717-97), the author of *The Castle of Otranto* (1764), the first Gothic novel, rebuilt Strawberry Hill House in the Gothic style in 1790. It was the fore-runner of the revival of the Gothic style building. In addition, the taste of the Middle Ages was enlivened by the English Romantic poets who emerged in the 19th century, and the trend of returning to the Middle Ages became the background of the Gothic Revival movement. After the Industrial Revolution in the 18th century, pragmatism and utilitarianism emerged, and many people stopped going to church. The Middle Ages were the age of Christianity. Some

Houses of Parliament in the morning

advocated for a return to the Middle Ages and wanted to revive the Golden Age of Christianity once again in the 19th century. The interpretation was that medieval architecture reflected the sincere Christian spirit of medieval architects who were devout Christians.

From Westminster Bridge

In fact, most of the castles that can be visited in England today, were rebuilt and restored during this period (Cardiff Castle and Castell Coch in Wales designed by William Burges are typical examples). At that time, in a society dominated by accelerating rationalism, there were a certain number of people who could not keep up with new ideas. They were conservatives and devout Christians. They supported the Gothic Revival, and their ideas spread to a certain number. In the 19th century, just before the Gothic Revival, many of London's public buildings used symmetrical Greek styles. However, in the latter half of the Victorian era (late 18th and 19th centuries), when the Gothic Revival movement flourished, many public buildings including churches and station buildings, were rebuilt as Gothic architecture (Neo-Gothic architecture). Westminster Palace is a prime example of this. The British Houses of Parliament were completed in 1852.

Big Ben, the symbol of London, is the 96.3-meter-high clock tower, completed in 1859. Its name was changed from "Clock Tower" to "Elizabeth Tower" in 2012 to commemorate the 60th anniversary of Queen Elizabeth II's reign, but it is commonly known as Big Ben. Big Ben is correctly the nickname of the bell installed in the clock tower, but it is used to refer to the big clock tower itself. The prevailing theory is that Big Ben was named after Sir

Benjamin Hall, a MP (Member of Parliament) who was in charge of the construction of the tower. Strangely enough, the sound of the bell that announces the time became popular throughout Japan after World War II, when a teacher at a school in Japan adopted the sound as the melody of the end-of-class chime. Big Ben is, of course, a representative landmark of London.

Today, a bronze statue of Prime Minister Churchill stands in Parliament Square. Sir Winston is holding his cane firmly in his right hand, and looking at Big Ben with a wry look on his face.

Sir Winston Churchill's Challenge

The natural forces are working with greater freedom and greater opportunity to fertilise and vary the thoughts and power of individual men and women. They are far bigger and more pliant in the vast structure of a mighty empire than could ever have been conceived by Marx in his hovel..... As long therefore as the free world holds together, and especially Britain and the United States, and maintains its strength, Russia will find that Peace and Plenty have more to offer than exterminatory war. The broadening of thought is a process which acquires momentum by seeking opportunity for all who claim it. And it may well be if wisdom and patience are practiced that Opportunity-for-All will conquer the minds and restrain the passions of mankind.[2]

Memoirs of The Second World War

Sir Winston Churchill, the grandson of the 7ᵗʰ Duke of Marlborough, was born in 1874 at Blenheim Palace in Oxfordshire, England. His father, Randolph, was a conservative politician, and his mother, Jennie, was American. Ever since he was a child, he hated studying and his grades were the lowest in all subjects. After graduating from the Royal Military Academy Sandhurst, while serving in various countries, he earned money by publishing *The Story of the Malakand Field Force* which was based on his war experiences in India. After that, it continued to be published and was well received. In 1899, he left the army to make a living by writing, and went to war as a private journalist. At the age of 26, he ran for the Conservative Party and was elected for the first time and entered politics. In

Statue of Churchill

1908, he became President of the Board of Trade. In the same year (age 33), he married Clementine Hozier, the daughter of Sir Henry (a British Army officer) and Lady Blanche. They had one son and three daughters. At the age of 35, he was promoted to Home Secretary, and when World War I began, he became the First Lord of the Admiralty (the head of the British Royal Navy), but was dismissed on the way. He served on the Western Front as a Major in the Army, and many of his troops were killed. In 1917, he was appointed as the Minister of Munitions and worked on the development of tanks to break through the trenches.

In November 1918, World War I ended. The following year, Churchill became both Secretary of State for War and Secretary of State for Air. Riots and strikes were frequent and red flags were raised here and there in the country. Communist currents quickly became mainstream in many regions. The possibility that Britain would become a communist state, increased. Under such circumstances, Churchill devoted himself to anti-communist diplomacy. Churchill, who was too radical, was transferred to the post of Secretary of State for the Colonies in 1921. In the general election of 1922, he was considered a belligerent politician and lost his Dundee seat. Around this time, he wrote *The World Crisis*. He lost again in the next election. In 1924, he became Chancellor of the Exchequer and was a leading candidate for the next prime minister. When Mussolini of Italy rose to power, Churchill commented that "Fascism is the most effective antidote to the poison of Leninism, the Russian Revolution." In 1929, the Wall Street Crash doubled the number of unemployed people in the United Kingdom. His autobiography, *My Early Life*, was published in 1930. On September 1, 1939, German forces invaded Poland, and finally on September 3, 1939, Britain and France declared war on Germany. World War II began, and Churchill was appointed First Lord of the Admiralty.

Eventually, public opinion became dominated by the long-awaited view that Churchill should become prime minister. In 1940, the first Churchill cabinet began (at the age of 65). Churchill arrested fascists and communists in the country one after another. After the withdrawal of Dunkirk and the fierce battle of the British mainland called the Battle of Britain, the Normandy landings were successful on June 6, 1944. After the fall of Rome, Mussolini was captured and executed (April 28), then Italy surrendered on May 2, 1945. After Hitler's suicide (April 30), Germany surrendered on May 8, 1945. At last, Japan surrendered on August 14, 1945. Churchill eventually became a national hero. In 1951, he became prime minister again (at the age of 77), and appealed to the world the presence of Britain as the important country possessing the atomic bomb after the United States and the Soviet Union. From 1948, he wrote *Memoirs of the Second World War*, and in 1953 he was awarded the Nobel Prize in Literature. He resigned as prime minister in '55 and retired from politics. He collapsed from a stroke in 1965 and died a few days later at the age of 90, and a state funeral was held in London.

Churchill was Britain's most popular politician. He was the leader of Britain during World War II. After the rise of Hitler, while the countries of Europe bowed down to Nazism, Churchill insisted on fighting thoroughly. Britain struggled alone, fighting an all-out war, and finally won with American reinforcements. However, if we look closely at his military and political achievements, there is no record of his extraordinary leadership and miracles. He didn't have any special talent as a strategist. Victory was not always coming when he became commander. He would win or lose. He was entrusted with many ministerial positions, but sometimes he did well and sometimes his policy didn't work out. In a sense, he was just a leader. However, he was appointed minister again and again, sacked, and finally elected as a top wartime leader. He was thoroughly anti-communist, anti-German, and pro-American. He hated Gandhi for leading a nonviolent movement in India. Many British politicians of the time were sympathetic to Nazi Germany and were generous to Germany's demand for rearmament. The pro-Germans tried to use Germany as an anti-Soviet bulwark. Churchill, the eccentric, clearly maintained his anti-Nazist position instinctively and intuitively. Maybe he chose that option because of his sense of balance.

Churchill at Hellfire Corner

During World War II, Dover Castle served as a military command center and underground hospital. Even now, vestiges of the fierce war remain everywhere around the castle. Beneath the White Cliffs facing the sea near Cannon's Gate was a concrete balcony, one part of Hellfire Corner, where the British underground headquarters was located. I have visited there before. I thought of Churchill's failure of Norwegian Campaign in April, 1940, the birth of Churchill's cabinet in May, the withdrawal of Dunkirk at the end of the same month, and the surrender of France, and London Blitz (Blitzkrieg). It made Britain completely isolated and helpless, as Nazi Germany wished. On August 28, 1940, Winston Churchill came to inspect the base, and now several photographs in the corner show the scene.

Churchill in 1941

Sandwiched between two men wearing military uniforms, Prime Minister Churchill, wearing a polka-dot bow tie and a suit with vertical stripes, and putting on a round helmet, looked through binoculars into the Straits of Dover from the balcony. However, although it may be unscrupulous, Churchill's appearance did not convey any sense of urgency and seriousness. It was somehow charming, giving no impression that it was a photograph of a fierce battle with the Nazis. Between 1941 and 1965, the constable of Dover Castle was Churchill. As swayed on the train to London, I reflected on Churchill's agony at Hellfire Corner. The image of Churchill wearing a helmet and no military uniform became symbolically ingrained in my head even as time passed. Churchill, a small X-legged man with an obese body, wearing a polka-dot bow tie, and an iron helmet, was watching the dogfight (aerial battle) in the Straits of Dover through binoculars. The character of Prime Minister Churchill acting somewhat humorously in a desperate situation while raising the patriotism of the British people and tackling difficult situations shook my heart strongly.

4. The Tower of London and King Edward the First

A castle originally means "a fortified lord's house" and was the housing facility of the lord and his family with vassals in the Middle Ages. The basic structure of the castle is a bailey (basically two baileys) protected by a gate, drawbridge, moat (ditch) and wall. In the bailey, there are a main tower called a keep, a hall that is used for multiple purposes, and other strong buildings with living space. In the 11th century, the Normans brought a motte-and-bailey castle, the first fortified building called "castle" from the continent to England. Eventually, the castles changed from wood to stone, with white castles in the south of England made of limestone, and brick-colored castles built in the north

The White Tower (Tower of London) was completed in 1087

of the country, made of red sandstone. The main tower, called a keep, has two patterns: a square keep (rectangular keep) and a circular shell keep. A representative example of a square keep is the White Tower of the Tower of London and a shell keep is the Round Tower of Windsor Castle.

二年の留学中只一度倫敦塔を見物した事がある。その後再び行こうと思った日もあるが止めにした。人から誘われた事もあるが断った。⁽³⁾

夏目漱石「倫敦塔」

During my two years studying abroad, I visited the Tower of London once. After that, there were days when I wanted to go again, but I stopped. I was once invited to go to the castle by someone, but I refused.

The Tower of London is the most representative royal castle in England. Its official name is "His Majesty's Royal Palace and Fortress of the Tower of London". For Japanese, it is also familiar from Natsume Soseki's short story 'Tower of London' (1905). It is a tourist attraction that many people who come to England will visit at least once. This castle is called just "Tower", but it is a well-established castle, and it is still the royal fortifications of Charles III. There are guards sent to guard the royal residence. William, Duke of Normandy, who had conquered England like a fury, feared the resistance of the Anglo-Saxons who had settled in the area, and intended to build a castle in London to protect his family and his vassals. When the Norman Duke William was crowned King of England, he immediately built the castle by making good use of some of the ruins of the Roman Fort, which had been built during Roman rule. William was the first in England to build a castle. It was a wooden castle with a ditch around it, and surrounded by a timber fence. Eventually, William the Conqueror planned to build a stone rectangular keep (tower) in the center of the castle as a palace to show his wealth and power. After the king's death, his son William II completed the stone keep in 1078. Initially, the keep was called the Tower (of London), but later, as the castle area expanded until around 1400, this keep (tower) was called the White Tower because of its white-washed appearance, and the entire castle came to be called the Tower of London. This is why only this castle is called the Tower of London, which should have been called London Castle. The stone walls of the White Tower are actually white. They were made of milky white limestone called Kent stone. In addition, the walls were coated with lime paint. It was not just because of the beautiful appearance, but because it had the effect of preventing the stone walls from deterioration. Successive kings made the Tower of London a stronger castle and expanded each time townspeople and peasants demanded tax cuts and rebelled. In the 12th century, Richard I and his brother, King John, built the outer walls of the castle, doubling its total area.

The Round Tower of Windsor Castle in England

Edward I, King of the Castle Builder

King Edward I (1239-1307) was a king who built many splendid castles in Wales. His castles were very important in the history of European castles. And of course, he was also enthusiastic about the expansion of the Tower of London. The King filled the moat with earth in his father's time and dug new moats to

King Edward I

provide double protection. Many of the castles built by Edward I were the latest of the time, called concentric castles, but they are also called Edwardian castles, in honor of the king's name. They were square castles with two sets of curtain walls, and the inner wall was higher than the outer enclosing wall. Soldiers could shoot, from the inner wall, the enemies over the outer wall. Even if enemies broke through the first wall, they were forced to stand in a small space and were greeted by arrow-attacks. The Tower of London was also converted into a concentric castle at this time.

Edward I was born in the Palace of Westminster as the eldest son of Henry III. The height of the king was 190 cm. He was intelligent, and a good speaker in public. His hair was blonde in childhood, dark brown in adulthood, and white like a swan in his later years. Even after reaching old age, his muscles were tight, his agile movements did not decline, and he was a brave king who always led his army to the front line himself and struggled, and he never suffered from illness during his life. The King listened well to the opinions of the nobility, while increasing the power of the English King. When he was a prince, Edward crossed the continent for a crusading expedition. He heard of the death of his father Henry III, in Italy on his way back from Palestine, and hurriedly returned to England, where he was crowned King of England in 1272. In 1295, King Edward summoned the Great Council (Parliament) for the first time at Westminster Hall, which became the first representative parliament and a model for later generations (Model Parliament). Among the Plantagenet kings, he was the greatest leader since Henry II, and in the context of the Anglo-Norman English royal family on the verge of collapse, Edward was a so-called trump card that appeared after his undesired grandfather King John and his father Henry III. The first wife of Edward was Eleanor of Castile (1241-1290), princess of the Kingdom of Castile. She gave birth to Edward of Caernarfon (the first English Prince of Wales). King Edward loved his Queen so much that when she died, he had 12 cross-towers (Eleanor crosses) erected at every place her funeral cortege stopped on its way to London. The second wife of King Edward was Margaret of France (1279-1318), a daughter of Philip III of France. At that time, Edward was 60 years old, and Margaret was only 21 years old. Two sons and one girl were born between them.

This outstanding Edward I of England was also highly regarded as a castle-builder. English castles of the 13th and 14th centuries, built by King Edward, including 14 castles in Wales (Caernarfon Castle, Conwy Castle, Harlech Castle, etc.), were known for representing the strong castles of medieval Europe. King Edward abandoned ancestral continental territories which were lost by his grandfather King John, and considered that the first priority was the conquest of

Wales and Scotland, that is, the complete unification of the entire island of Britain. Edward convened Parliament and promised not to raise taxes without Parliament's consent. He first aimed to stabilize domestic politics in England, and he was committed to economic development, encouraging trade and industry. When the time was ripe, he launched wars of aggression against Wales (1277-1282) and Scotland (1296-1307).

Margaret of France

Harlech Castle in Wales

King Edward's invasion of Wales left considerable brutality scars, and as a result, he built fortifications along the coastline, including Flint Castle, Rhuddlan Castle, Conwy Castle, Beaumaris Castle, Caernarfon Castle, Criccieth Castle, Harlech Castle, Castell Y Bere, and Aberystwyth Castle. It was a policy of occupation by a network of castles devised to show the military might of England and to hold the breath of the Welsh rebellion. King Edward's policy or strategy to control Wales against raiders, was very similar to the occupation policy of William I (William the Conqueror), who built a number of motte-and-bailey castles in various places in England and made them safe residences and administrative bases for Norman barons (feudal lords). Just like William the Conqueror, Edward I built many strong castles in Wales as military bases for complete conquest of Wales.

The concentric castle, also known as the Edwardian castle, was the result of the development of the castle-building techniques that King Edward learned during his Crusader expedition to the Holy Land of Palestine in 1270-1272, as well as his deep knowledge of European castles. Of course, Edward ordered master mason, Master James of St. George, to build many castles. But it seems that the King himself was quite skilled in castle construction, and he chose the castle site himself, and instructed the construction of the castle as much as possible. The concentric castle built by King Edward is said to be modeled after the Syrian concentric castle, "Krak des Chevaliers", but Edward's sense of castle construction was fully utilized and it became the highest standard of military fortress at that time in Europe. Conventionally, the keep was the strongest point of the castle, and the gate was the weakest against the attack of the castle. In the concentric type castle, the function of the keep, the last defense base of the castle, was applied to the castle gate. Even allowing enemy soldiers to break through the gate and to attack inside the castle, the upper part of the gatehouse (keep gatehouse) would still serve as a control tower. Here, the castle's biggest weakness was transformed into the strongest military facility. After all, the concentric castle was the pinnacle of medieval castles, and its geometric shape also led to later bastion military fortifications (such as Deal Castle in England), which also served as a bridge between medieval castles and early modern military fortifications.

In addition, the value of plastic beauty of the concentric castle is very high; there are many well-proportioned ones made by King Edward. What is fundamentally different from the traditional English castles that had developed from motte-and-bailey is the layout. The conventional castle was built to make the most of the natural terrain as much as possible, and of course, the structure of the castle was not symmetrical and had an irregular composition. Since the scale of the castle constantly expanded, its layout became complex and diverse. The buildings were chaotic as a whole. As a result, it became a heavy Gothic architectural castle rich in variety. However, the concentric castle had no such irregularities. Every castle was built rationally, and the building was symmetrical, well-proportioned, and well-balanced. Its appearance seemed like a geometric design. At the same

Caernarfon Castle in Wales

The Tower of London is a representative of British castles

time, by effectively arranging large and small towers, turrets, and gatehouses, it kept enough Gothic heaviness and strength. Thus, a well-fortified medieval castle, suddenly emerged in the desolate Welsh wilderness. It was a miracle worthy of the end-of-life beauty of the history of medieval castles.

In 1294-5, there was a serious rebel uprising in Wales and many castles were attacked. In a hurry, King Edward sent a large army to Wales to suppress the rebels. Although Welsh independence was prevented, Edward was confused by many problems in his last years. The problem of financial difficulties, the French Gascony Dispute, the Scottish Problem, the Irish Problem, the domestic ecclesiastical taxation issue, and the rise of anti-war views were all problems that the King was struggling with, without finding any effective solution. As for the complete conquest of Scotland, it was prevented by the resistance of Robert Bruce and William Wallace, even with the army of Edward I, which was said to be the strongest in the world. Furthermore, Scotland allied with France against England. In fact, it was planned to build a number of concentric castles on the Scottish coastline, just like Wales. However, in the end, it was not realized due to lack of funds. The failure of the conquest of Scotland was not only due to the incompetence of King Edward's son, Edward II, nor to the fact that Scotland had more heroes, or patriots than Wales, but rather that England did not have the funds to build a robust network of castles. In 1307, King Edward decided to go to Scotland, to suppress the rebels instigated by Robert Bruce who had ascended to the throne of King Robert I of Scotland. Despite suffering from dysentery, King Edward I went out to defeat Robert Bruce, and died in the northern England during the advance.

If you have enough time to visit the castle, I recommend taking a leisurely walk around the castle. Castles in England were built in one era and have not been preserved ever since, but have been renovated and expanded afterwards. So, even the same castle has various expressions. Even if you look at one photo of the castle, compared to another shot taken from a different angle, it is unimaginable that they are the same castle photos. The Tower of London is one of such castles, and if you go around the castle, you will find the Tower of London with various faces that make you feel the era, such as the ruins of the Roman Fort, the Norman keep, the square tower, the round tower, the royal palace, the curtain wall, the concentric castle, the military fortress, the battery, and barracks. Everything coexists without being destroyed.

5. London Bridge and Tower Bridge

I was often up at six o'clock, and that my favorite lounging-place in the interval was old London Bridge, where I was wont to sit in one of the stone recesses, watching the people going by, or to look over the balustrades at the sun shining in the water, and lighting up the golden flame on the top of the Monument.[4]

David Copperfield

The first bridge over the River Thames was London Bridge. The history of London Bridge dates back to 46 AD. The Romans, who ruled England at the

Houses once lined Old London Bridge

time, built the first wooden bridge over the Thames. Its location was slightly different from the current location. Later, a new wooden bridge was built in the Anglo-Saxon era. In the 12th century, during the reign of King John, the wooden bridge was replaced with a robust stone bridge. The purpose was not only to show the majesty of the walled city of London, but also to protect the City (of London) preparing for emergencies. First, it was necessary to stop the enemy from attacking across the river from the opposite bank of the south even if there was an economic need for north-south traffic. It was also

Current London Bridge

One of piers of London Bridge

necessary to have a barrier to stop enemy warships (large ships) from entering the heart of London up to the inner Thames from the sea. Therefore, a drawbridge was installed on the south side of the bridge. In general, the drawbridge installed on the bridge was made to block its passage of bridge. Just in case enemies attack from the south, a part of the bridge is chained up to prevent them from entering. But as for London Bridge, it could also stop large ships passing through the river under the bridge. The drawbridge could be used to raise part of the bridge with a chain to pass large ships coming up the Thames, and if they didn't want them to pass, they could lower the chain. In addition, as a defense against intruders crossing from the south side of the bridge, a gatehouse with a portcullis was built at the south end. In a broad sense, Old London Bridge was part of the castle, the Tower of London.

The general supervisor of the work was Peter de Colechurch. He formally advocated the construction of the Sacred London Bridge and aimed to complete a 300-meter-long, 7-meter-wide stone bridge consisting of 20 arches (19 sturdy piers). Of course, Priest Peter did not want the construction of this stone bridge to be for military purposes only. Shops (and houses) were to be lined up on the bridge (which also made the bridge more defensive), but the most notable was that he wanted to build the chapel dedicated to St Thomas of Canterbury, commemorating Thomas Becket's martyrdom (renamed St Mary's Chapel after Henry VIII's Reformation).

The idea of building a chapel on a bridge is said to have emerged in the late Middle Ages. It was an attempt to realize a beautiful abode of God on a bridge. At the same time, it would have had a religious connotation of protecting the bridge by God. The morale of the workers involved in the actual construction of the bridge must have been raised. Finally, the holy small chapel was built on the north side of the bridge, near the City. The bridge, taking 33 years, was completed in 1209. Unfortunately, Priest Peter died of illness three years before the bridge was completed. His body was buried in the basement of the chapel of St Thomas on the bridge. When the chapel was demolished in the 19th century, the white skeletal remains of the priest were reportedly exhumed.

In the 14th century, there were more than 130 shops (and houses) on the bridge. There were bakeries, shoe shops, tailors, liquor stores, bookstores, hardware stores, blacksmiths, haberdashery shops, general stores, etc. It is estimated that more than 600 people lived on the bridge, and the bridge was just like a floating city. Passers-by on the bridge were subject to a toll tax. However, the tax was limited to going from the Southwark side to the City. The tax money was used to pay for the maintenance and repair of the bridge and the chapel.

Thomas More, The Last Resistance

It's unbelievable today, but many heads of political prisoners or heads of rebels were exposed over the bridge in the past. In fact, most of them were skewered, hoisted and exposed on top of the gatehouse on the south side of the bridge. It is said that Sir William Wallace was the first to be exposed in 1305. These included Wat Tyler in 1381, Thomas More in 1535, and Thomas Cromwell, 1st Earl of Essex in 1540. This notorious custom for traitors was abolished in 1660 with the restoration of Charles II.

Sir Thomas More (1478-1535) was a lawyer, judge, scholar, author, and a man of great faith. He studied at Oxford University and then at the London Law Institute, becoming a barrister. In 1516, he published *Utopia*, written in Latin. He wrote a fictional ideal society using the word Utopia, which word was coined by More. He married at the age of 27 and was blessed with three daughters and a son. He was eventually recognized by Henry VIII and in 1529 became Lord High Chancellor of England, the highest-ranking chancellor in the bureaucracy.

However, he stood for the cause of faith and justice as Lord Chancellor, and was at odds with King Henry over King's divorce issue. More was accused of treason and

Henry VIII

Sir Thomas More

sent to the Tower of London. Then, he was executed at Westminster Hall. Shortly before execution, More said to the beheading officer, "I have a beard now, but it is innocent, not guilty. Please don't cut off this beard." I think this story shows the characteristics of the British. It doesn't have much to do with whether or not his beard is cut off or not. He was to be killed because he disobeyed King Henry's wishes. When he was told to die, he could not resist anything. But the point is that it is not good to be told to die and not resist and then be executed silently. It is important to show some resistance to anything. Human beings need an attitude of resisting at any cost. You should say something back when you are hopeless. You should assert yourself until the very end, so that your point will be accepted even a little bit no matter what. The attitude of not giving up until the last minute can lead to a breakthrough.

More's head was stabbed with a stick and exposed on London Bridge. After 30 days of exposure, his daughter Margaret, secretly gave the money to the keeper of London Bridge, before the head was dumped into the Thames. His head was later buried on the altar of St Dunstan's Church, Canterbury.

Later Old London Bridge

London Bridge is broken (falling) down,
Broken (falling) down, broken (falling) down,
London Bridge is broken (falling) down,
My fair lady.

It is not clear when this song (nursery rhyme) began to be sung. But at least, it would have been popular as late as the 18th century. This song suggested the

medieval Old London Bridge, which had
been restored many times but was about
to reach the limit of its durability and
was on the verge of physical collapse. At
the same time, the meaning of "London
Bridge is falling down" implied the
historical fact that the "Holy Bridge"
that Peter de Colechurch had poured all
his heart into had collapsed.

London Bridge and the Shard (right)

The construction of the second bridge over the Thames in London, named
Westminster Bridge, began in 1739 and was completed in 1750. Blackfriars Bridge
was built in 1760. London Bridge was extensively renovated in 1758-62, and all
houses on the bridge were removed. However, the piers were noticeably
dilapidated, and the bridge had reached its limit. Parliament in Westminster
decided to build a new bridge, which was entrusted to John Rennie (1761-1821), a
Scottish civil engineer. Designed by Rennie, a new marble bridge consisting of
five arches on four piers was planned, which was actually completed in 1831 by
Rennie's son. Waterloo Bridge (1811-17) and Southwark Bridge (1813-19) were
also built by John Rennie. Construction of the current London Bridge began in
1967 by Architect John Mowlem (1788-1868) and in 1973, the opening ceremony
was held with Queen Elizabeth II seated next to him. The new stone bridge is very
simple with three arches and a six-lane carriageway flanked by five-meter-wide
sidewalks on both sides.

Tower Bridge, a masterpiece of Neo-Gothic Architecture

During the Victorian era, the Gothic Revival flourished, and the representative

65-meter-high tower

example is the rebuilt Houses of Parliament in Westminster, but other representative buildings are the restored Tower of London and the newly built Tower Bridge. It is a drawbridge with two medieval Gothic towers, built in 1894. In the late 19th century, the commercial development of the East End necessitated another new bridge downstream of London Bridge. However, between London Bridge and the Tower of London, the Pool of London, a wharf where many large ships docked, was located on both sides of the Thames, and large ocean-going ships could enter there. The current Upper Pool is the former Pool of London, and now the Lower Pool is further downstream. It extends from Tower Bridge to Cherry Garden Pier. At that time, a fixed bridge could not be built to avoid obstacles to the entry of large ships coming to the dock. This led to the invention of the drawbridge. The bridge is 244 meters long, the Gothic towers on the left and right are 65 meters high, and there is a historical museum inside the bridge. Because it creates a castle-like landscape, it is now said to be the most beautiful bridge in the world.

Tower Bridge can be opened and closed as two main towers monitor ships passing through the Thames. In a sense, the Tower of London had a military significance to keep an eye on enemy ships attacking up the Thames from the continent. William the Conqueror therefore built a castle on the far left of the City to protect the town. Now, Tower Bridge would have that implication. The Tower of London and Tower Bridge are also in harmony with each other. If you read deeply, in a sense, Tower Bridge can be interpreted as enhancing the Tower of London's function as a castle. In the Middle Ages, when the stone London Bridge was built, it would have served to stop the passage of foreign ships into the depths of London. Newly built Tower Bridge was, in every sense, inevitable. The Palace of Westminster on the west and Tower Bridge on the east end, hold London firmly on the left and right. The idea of building two castle-like structures on both sides of the bridge may have been influenced by the medieval Old London Bridge, where a chapel, gatehouse, and shops were built on the bridge and lined up.

Currently, between the Tower of London and London Bridge on the River Thames, the Royal Navy cruiser Belfast floats as a memorial ship. The interior is now a floating museum. I feel that this is a remnant of the military importance of this area in the past, and when I see a Navy ship floating on the water, I still feel a sense of tension for a moment. This ship must also hint at something.

Tower Bridge completed in 1894

6. The British Museum and the Great People

The stunning main entrance, reminiscent of a Greek Temple, was built in 1848 and is said to be the largest classical style architecture in London. Exactly 270 years ago (1753), the opening of the British Museum was approved by the Westminster Parliament next to King George II. It was the age of

Main entrance of the museum

Enlightenment. The former Duke of Montagu's mansion (Montagu House) in present-day Bloomsbury was bought and prepared for opening, and the oldest and largest museum in history was officially opened to the public on January 15, 1759. It started with two departments, the Library Department and the Museum Department dealing with historical archaeology, folklore, etc. (The British Library was not completely separated from the British Museum until 1997). In 1823, King George IV donated the books (over 65,000 volumes) inherited from his father, George III, and a specially built gallery called the King's Library, was added to the British Museum (now moved and turned into an exhibition room). In 1857, a round reading room, officially named British Museum Reading Room, was built in the central part of the courtyard.

To commemorate the millennium of 2000, the circular dome of the former Reading Room was reborn as the Great Court, an all-white beautiful space, designed by Norman Forster (1935-). Admission fee has been free since its opening. Even the staff of the ushers are never allowed to accept tips, which continues to this day. Charging has been discussed many times, but the idea has always disappeared. Considering 6.5 million visitors a year, even an entrance fee of £1 per person would be a substantial amount. Of course, the Louvre Museum in France charges a fee. British Museum has 94 exhibition rooms and 150,000 exhibits. The collection includes about 7 million items. Most of the items in the collection are donated by private collectors. Others were donated by various foundations, excavated and discovered by museum surveys, and purchased with the state budget, not taken from the former colonies.

A museum born from Sir Hans Sloane's hobby

The British Museum is a museum established based on the collection of about 70,000 items by a private physician, Sir Hans Sloane (1660-1753). Hans was born into an Anglo-Irish family in Northern Ireland. His father, Alexander Sloane, was a trustee of the nobility, who died when Hans was six years old. Although he was prone to illness, Hans was a curious and knowledgeable boy as a child. The boy eventually became interested in medicine, obtained a doctorate in medicine from a French university (the University of Orange-Nassau), and upon his return began practicing medicine in the Bloomsbury area of London (later near the British Museum). Later, he went to Jamaica to accompany the new Governor of Jamaica as a personal physician, where he recorded 800 species of plants. They were catalogued in Latin, and later he published *Catalogue of Jamaican Plants* in 1696. While in Jamaica, Sloane

Great Court

Sir Hans Sloane

discovered that chocolate (cocoa) is easy to drink when mixed with milk. He eventually became a royal doctor and served Queen Anne, George I, and George II. In 1716 (aged 56), he became a baronet, called "Sir Hans". In 1727, he became the first physician to King George II. When he retired in 1741, he acquired several collections one after another from various collectors. Sir Hans' manor house of Chelsea had such a huge amount of collections and books, that it was called the "Museum & Library". In 1753, when he died, he wrote in his will that he would donate his entire collections to Parliament in exchange for paying £20,000 to his family. Hans' day job was a doctor, and the collection was just his hobby. He donated his collections to the British government, which later became the British Museum.

Sir William Hamilton

Collections of Sir William Hamilton

Another man credited with developing the early British Museum was Sir William Hamilton (1730-1803). He was born as the fourth son of the prestigious Scottish nobleman, Lord Archibald Hamilton, governor of Jamaica. Hamilton grew up with, and served the Prince of Wales (later George III) from an early age. It is said that the prince would call him his "foster brother". Hamilton became an army officer, and married at the age of

25. In 1761(age 31), became a Member of Parliament. When he heard the position of ambassador in Naples was going to be vacant, he expressed an interest in the position, and at the age of 34, became British Ambassador to the Kingdom of Naples (1764-1800). He had a taste for classicism and began collecting antiquities in Naples. He bought Greek and Roman vases, sculptures, coins, armor helmets, and stone busts. Hamilton's collections grew to about 7,000 pieces. In 1772, they were transported to England and the British Museum bought them in bulk. They became the largest collections owned by the British Museum since its opening. In 1784, Hamilton donated his subsequent collections of Greek and Roman antiquities to the British Museum again.

The charm of Rosetta Stone

Speaking of exhibits at the British Museum, Rosetta Stone, which often appears in world history and English textbooks in Japan, is probably the foremost. It is on display in an ancient Egyptian gallery. In 1799, when Napoleon Bonaparte (1769-1821) led his army on an expedition to Egypt, Lieutenant Pierre-François discovered a 762-kilogram granite megalith in Rosetta, the Nile Delta. It was confirmed that the stone was a monument of an edict issued by one of Egyptian kings in 196 BC. At that time, the French army was accompanied by a large number of archaeologists during the Egyptian expedition, who collected art and artifacts from ancient Egypt and brought them back to France (they were largely returned to Egypt in 1816 after Napoleon's defeat). The Rosetta Stone was naturally supposed

Rosetta Stone

to be brought back to France, but the French were defeated by the British who landed in Egypt, and in 1801, the Rosetta Stone was handed over to the British. The reason why this megalith is so important is that the surface of the stone monument was engraved with three different types of languages. That is: ancient Egyptian characters, Egyptian folk characters, and Greek characters. Because the same content was written in three different scripts, it was possible for the first time to decipher the ancient Egyptian hieroglyphs that no one had understood before.

As a result, ancient Egyptology made a phenomenal academic development. The magnitude of the academic value of this stone is even romantic. In 1802, under the direction of King George III, the stone was donated to the British Museum and opened to the public. Since then, it has been the most popular exhibit to this day. Meanwhile, since 2003, when the British Museum celebrated its 250th anniversary, Egypt has been asking for the stone to be returned. Does this come to a conclusion? For example, what about acknowledging that the stone is owned by Egypt and displaying it at the British Museum with Egypt's consent? This will make more people around the world more interested in and know the ancient Egyptian civilization.

Parthenon Marbles sparks the poet's imagination

It was in August 1816 that the British government purchased the Parthenon Marbles (known as the Elgin Marbles, a collection of Ancient Greek sculptures from the Parthenon and others) and placed them in the British Museum. At the end of the 18th century, Turkish ambassador Thomas Bruce, 7th Earl of Elgin (1766-1841), worried about the devastation of the Parthenon (the ancient Temple of the Idols), invested £70,000 in his personal fortune and later sold it

to the British Museum for £35,000. One day, the painter Benjamin Robert Haydon (1786-1846) invited John Keats (1795-1821), a young Romantic poet who had just made his debut, to show these splendid sculptures. Genius Keats was exposed to authentic Greek antiquities or figurative beauty. Then Keats awakened to universal beauty. It was shortly after Keats published his first collection of poems. Keats' most famous narrative poem *Endymion* (1818) was written after seeing the Marble figure of Endymion sleeping on Mount Latmos, on display as part of the Townley's collection of Greek and Roman sculptures.

John Keats

A THING of beauty is a joy for ever:
Its loveliness increases; it will never
Pass into nothingness; but still will keep
A bower quiet for us, and a sleep
Full of sweet dreams, and health, and quiet breathing.[5]

Endymion Book I, lines 1-5

Keats visited the British Museum again in 1819 to write 'Ode on a Grecian Urn'.

O Attic shape! Fair attitude! with brede
Of marble men and maidens overwrought,
With forest branches and the trodden weed;

Thou, silent form! dost tease us out of thought

As doth eternity: Cold Pastoral!

When old age shall this generation waste,

Thou shalt remain, in midst of other woe

Than ours, a friend to man, to whom thou say'st,

'Beauty is truth, truth beauty'— that is all

Ye know on earth, and all ye need to know.[6]

'Ode on a Grecian Urn'

Many of Keats' poems deal with the theme of beauty, and he was described as a "martyr of beauty". Keats often sought Greek mythology as a subject, leaving these words, "A thing of beauty is a joy forever" (*Endymion*) and "Beauty is truth, truth beauty" (*Ode on a Grecian Urn*). Keats died in Rome at the age of 25.

The British Library that Dickens loved

Charles Dickens

The British Museum and the British Library were located on the same site. However, in 1997, the library was relocated and the splendid Reading Room was gone. The former Reading Room was so popular with its wonderful circular dome-shaped roof, and it was used by various great people. For example, Thomas Gray (1716-71), Sir Walter Scott (1771-1832), Charles Lamb (1775-1834), Charles Darwin (1809-1882, famous for his book *On the Origin of Species* about evolution),

Charles Dickens (1812-70), Thomas Hardy (1840-1928), George Bernard Shaw (1856-1950, after his death, he donated one-third of his property to the museum), and Sir Arthur Conan Doyle (1859-1930), etc.

Many Victorian writers who had visited the library, wrote many articles for newspapers and magazines. When the serialized work in the magazine was completed, they put them together and published a book. Magazines and books were established as products for the general public. Middle-class people became very powerful, and they were hungry for knowledge. Victorian writers needed to educate them because sometimes they were very utilitarian and money-minded. Novelists entertained people, and at the same time they played the role of making people think deeply about life. The Victorian era was the heyday of the novel, and Dickens was the most influential national writer among them.

> Marley was dead: to begin with. There is no doubt whatever about that. The register of his burial was signed by the clergyman, the clerk, the undertaker, and the chief mourner. Scrooge signed it: and Scrooge's name was good upon 'Change, for anything he chose to put his hand to. Old Marley was as dead as a door-nail.[7]
>
> *A Christmas Carol*

Dickens' writing style is characterized by detailed descriptions and rich psychological descriptions of characters. He was also good at writing sentences that made a lot of use of contrasts and repetitions to leave an impression on the reader. In addition, it is also known as a representative of social novels because it depicts social problems and sincerely depicts people's hardships and misery. Dickens' works continue to be loved all over the world for their stylistic

59

characteristics that are extremely easy to read and depict a deep humanity. *A Christmas Carol* is a novella published in 1843 by Dickens. It tells the story of Scrooge, an elderly miser, who meets the ghost of his business partner Marley, who died on Christmas Eve, and Old Scrooge travels and is converted by spirits of the past, present, and future.

A Christmas Carol is still most well-read by people all over the world, and it's the most famous work of Dickens'. However, I think *David Copperfield*, a large-scale novel in the bildungsroman genre with a strong autobiographical element, is a true masterpiece. Its writing style has many characteristics. First, the depiction is very detailed, vividly depicting the impression of the scene and the person. For example, an episode depicting Copperfield's boyhood is realistic and allows readers to empathize with his experience. In addition, the psychological descriptions of various characters are elaborately expressed, and the image of each character emerges graphically. For example, the portrayals of Mr. Edward Murdstone (Copperfield's strict father-in-law), Clara Peggotty (a loving nanny), Ham (sincere young man), Emily (an orphan), arrogant and ruthless James Steerforth, generous couple Mr. and Mrs. Micawber who live a life full of troubles, nervous but kind-hearted great-aunt Miss Betsey Trotwood, hypocrite clerk Uriah Heep, innocent and angelic first wife Dora, and intelligent second wife Agnes, are all particularly impressive, and their vivid characters leave a deep impression on the reader. Also, reflecting the growth process of Copperfield, the writing style also changes. The early years are somewhat archaic in writing, with more modern touches added in the second half. In this way, Dickens' writing style is characterized by having a variety of methods of expression according to its content.

Dickens' work features a variety of female figures. Among them, there are especially many women who are portrayed as chaste wives, who often support the emotions of male characters. They have virtues and beliefs, and lovingly protect their homes. On the other hand, women at the bottom of society suffer from poverty, exploitation, and are sometimes sexually abused. There are also many sociable and philanthropic women who find joy in interacting with people from diverse social strata and helping others. But sometimes they are stupid, vanity, and narrow-minded. Dickens portrayed women from multiple perspectives, creating a realistic depiction of them as they face social difficulties or troubles in relationships. Dickens also had a message of supporting women's rights and appealing for enlightenment in his work. His work also confronted the situation and discrimination of women in British society at the time.

Das Kapital. Kritik der politischen Ökonomie was born at the British Museum

Another great man, the philosopher Karl Marx, who proposed the idea that profoundly changed the state system of the world, also wrote his book *Das Kapital* (*Capital: Critique of Political Economy*) at the British Library.

Karl Marx was born in 1818, in Trier, a territory of the Kingdom of Prussia. His father came from a family of generational Jewish priests, but he was a liberal and converted to Protestantism, making a living as a lawyer. Marx's mother was Dutch-Jewish, and the Marx family was wealthy. He studied law, philosophy, literature and history at the Universities of Bonn and Berlin. In 1841, he received his doctorate in philosophy. Because he could not become a university professor, he became the editor-in-chief of a newspaper company, which eventually fell out of print. But Marx who had married the daughter of a Prussian nobleman four years older than him, moved to Paris with his wife and became involved in the running of the magazine's first issue. However, it was discontinued in the first issue, and although he subsequently contributed numerous articles to the journal, Marx was expelled from the country due to his critical views of the government and moved to Brussels, Belgium. In 1849, he fled to England and studied economics at the British Museum. He died in London in 1883, at the age of 64.

Marx regarded capital as a common asset of society and the workers who multiplied that capital as agents of social change. The Prussian government was wary of Marx because he was a dangerous revolutionary thinker who aimed for a society of equality without a gap between the rich and the poor, eliminating the distinction between capitalists (the bourgeoisie) who exploited surplus value and workers (the proletariat) who were exploited. Traditionally, it was thought that spiritual things moved history, but Marx taught that material things, the development of productive forces, make history. This way of thinking is called "historical materialism". Marx argued that capitalist society would eventually come to an end, and that the era of socialism and communism would come in the future.

Marx was a philosopher of "materialism", who held that everything in this world was ordained by matter, and that there was no such thing as God, the soul, the afterlife, or Ideas. In other words, it's the idea that there is only matter in the world. Since the reason for everything in this world is in matter, "justice" and "emotion" in the human mind are also determined by matter. For example, eating delicious food makes the human mind happy because of the substance of delicious food. If you get angry when you're beaten, it's the substance of the fist that creates anger in your heart. Also, suppose that people in a certain country live by catching fish from the sea, and the idea that "you should not catch too much

fish" is correct there. That correctness is not a
universal truth that is available anywhere in this
universe. There is a reason for the substance that if
you catch too much fish and destroy the marine
ecosystem, you will have trouble eating.

And, of course, Marx thought that the morality
of "do not tell a lie", the ethics that "human life
must be valued the most", the religion that "if you
believe in God, you will be saved", and the virtue
of "do not take revenge even if you are damaged",

Philosopher, Karl Marx

are all things that matter prescribes. Moreover,
the ruling class of the nation can manipulate matter at will, using money and
power. To be able to manipulate matter as they wish, means to be able to
determine the morals, ethics, religious teachings, and justice of a country in
their own favor. For example, what about the teachings of religion? "The rich
go to hell because they are wicked, and the poor go to heaven because they are
good. Under heaven all men are equal." If it is true that you can make it easier
in the other world because of the hardship in this world, you will be able to
keep the balance. But from the perspective of "materialism", there is no such
thing as the other world. Isn't the point that it is a convenient teaching for the
ruling class to force the poor to work hard for low wages by saying that they
can make it easier in a non-existent heaven because they work and struggle
pretty hard in this world? According to Marx's thinking, it can be interpreted as
follows. There is no God. That is why we create equality not with God, but with
the power of man. Then, how can we create equality? Marx cited Hegel's
"dialectics" and arranged it. The relationship between management and labor is

63

contradicted by the productive forces that improve with the development of the economy. In other words, even though the company's profits are rising, workers' wages remain the same. Therefore, the disgruntled workers wage a struggle against the ruling class, and working conditions will be improved. Thus, humanity advances by the class struggle that arises whenever contradictions arise. Therefore, Marx concluded that if the workers of the whole world united to start a revolution, they would be able to create an ideal socialist country in which all people were equal to each other.

However, we learned that when it came to socialism, the motivation to work declined, and the economy of one socialist country stagnated. In addition, shortcomings such as the danger of becoming a one-party state, a dictatorship, or not being able to freely make political statements were pointed out. In modern times, especially in liberal countries, many people recognize Marxism as a dangerous idea. However, isn't it premature to underestimate Marx with this? Because when Hegel said that humanity has progressed in "dialectics", Marx is quite right. Modern capitalism is very different from pre-Marx capitalism. We will not force people to work hard for low wages, and the gap between the rich and the poor is not as severe as it was before. Capitalism, which advocates liberty, has united the good points of the two sides and resolved the contradictions in the face of the opposing idea of socialism that advocates equality. Therefore, in modern society, there is capitalism that combines freedom and equality. Maybe Marx had anticipated this. Every time a contradiction arises, it is resolved and mankind progresses. Then of course there must be a contradiction in the socialism that he insisted. And there will be contradictions in modern capitalism at some point. In what Hegel says, there will be no contradictions in an ideal world that realizes true freedom. But it is a story of an endless future. Marx's assertion that a socialist country is an ideal country may have been a trick to motivate the workers to start a revolution.

It's a museum for great people from all over the world

There are many hobbyists in the UK. There are many British people whose hobbies different from their main business, reach the professional level. When I ask a British friend of mine, "What are your hobbies?", I am sometimes surprised by the high level of his or her hobbies. If it is a hobby, it is often a skill. If you say, "My hobby is painting", you are at a considerable level. Winston Churchill was also good at landscape painting. Sir Hans' hobby of collecting was devoted to amateurism until the end, but the museum that started from his collection is now the best museum in the world, attracting people from all over the world. It's just a hobby, but the level is professional. Isn't it very British? The fact that the British Museum does not charge an entrance fee may be related to the fact that it is originally a collection of an amateur ordinary citizen.

Originally, starting by showing a private collection to the general public, the British Museum inspired Josiah Wedgwood (1730-95) to duplicate the Portland Vase (completed in 1790), and nurtured the genius poet Keats or the great novelist Dickens to create their masterpieces. Darwin, the scholar who wrote *On the Origin of Species*, also studied there, and then the British Museum gave birth to the German philosopher Marx's *Das Kapital* which greatly influenced the political landscape of the world thereafter.

7. The Globe Theatre and Shakespeare

Shakespeare's Globe Theatre

The Globe Theatre, which was rebuilt in 1997, is called "Shakespeare's Globe Theatre". It is located about 230 meters away from the original theater. Medieval plays performed the Passion of Christ and the miracles of the saints in churches and on the streets, but it was forbidden to build theaters in the City of London. Theaters were also considered a den of plagues. Most theaters were therefore built on the north side of the city wall and across the Thames in Southwark. The Rose Theatre (in 1587), the Swan Theatre (in 1596), and the Globe Theatre (in 1599) were all built in the Southwark area.

On the campus of Waseda University in Tokyo, there is a theater museum (modeled after The Fortune Theatre in London), which is a great reference for understanding what kind of structure the theater building was at that time.

Shall I compare thee to a summer's day?
Thou art more lovely and more temperate:
Rough winds do shake the darling buds of May,
And summer's lease hath all too short a date;
Sometime too hot the eye of heaven shines,
And often is his gold complexion dimmed;
And every fair from fair sometime declines,

By chance or nature's changing course untrimmed:[8]

Sonnet 18

The Renaissance began in Italy in the 14th century. Suddenly, the revival of classics blossomed as if cutting the weir of a long sleep of art and science. Until then, classics in ancient Greece and Rome (Latin) had been held down for a long time by the Christian view of the world. The Renaissance means "reproduction" or "revival" in French. But the meaning strongly suggests "human revival". The main theme was to affirm humanity, that is, humanism. Renaissance humanism was a bold and powerful one, as exemplified by Leonardo da Vinci (1452-1519), who was interested in all elements of humans. Unlike subsequent humanism, Renaissance people did not focus on human weakness. Italians got out of the pressure of the Christian worldview in the Middle Ages, and they welcomed this sense as a detonator of European civilization. Eventually, Galileo Galilei (1564-1642) who was born in Pisa, Italy, appeared. Galileo excelled in mathematics, physics, and astronomy. And also, with a telescope he discovered sunspots, Jupiter's four moons, and Saturn's rings. As a scientist, Galileo argued for Copernicus' heliocentric theory, which caused the repression from the Roman Church. Later, he discovered the fallen law, which led to Newton's law of universal gravitation. The famous "Experiment of the Leaning Tower of Pisa" is one of his experiments at that time. It is a strong human interest and scientific spirit that characterizes Europeans since the 16th century. After that, European countries were transitioning to modernized ones. Man changed his concern from "God" to "himself". People began to have a clear view of things, that is, a scientific spirit. In England, in the 14th century, influenced by European literature, Geffrey

Chaucer (1343?-1400) wrote *The Canterbury Tales*, which composition is the same as *Decameron* written by Boccaccio (1313-75). Chaucer introduced many interesting English characters, and Sir Thomas More (1478-1535) wrote *Utopia*. Then, Francis Bacon (1561-1626) published many philosophical books, saying "knowledge is power". And then, the playwright William Shakespeare (1564-1616) appeared like a brilliant star in the dark sky, becoming a representative of the Renaissance in England. Shakespeare has had a profound influence on the world of theater and literature. No great writer exceeding Shakespeare has come out afterwards. In the history of the English language, his English belongs to Early Modern English. However, it remains an enduring influence on the subsequent history of English for the future of the global language we are heading for.

Shakespeare's Language

If we are to list the characteristics of Shakespeare's English, we realize Shakespeare emphasized, as N. F. Blake states, "the sound, rhythm, rhetoric, and the general drift of a passage more important than the precise meaning of individual words or grammatically correct word order."[9] First, we'd like to mention the richness of his vocabulary. Also, contrasts are often used. Old

words are mixed with new words. Words with a negative image and words with a positive image appear repeatedly; in particular, such kind of skill appears frequently in his sonnets. In addition, linguistically, words that appeared in Shakespeare's works appeared for the

Inside of the theater first time in those days. It means

Shakespeare coined so many new words and expressions. There are many examples of Early Modern English. Most of them are compound words used in those days. There is a great possibility that Shakespeare created new words, or he just happened to use them. Then the expression became widely known. There are many words and phrases that are still used today, and some of them have become proverbs.

There are spelling differences in Shakespeare's editions of Quarto, Folio (1623), and Globe (1864). Even the same Quarto edition has different spellings between in the first edition of First Quarto (1597) and in the Second Quarto (1599). His works are interspersed with the spoken language of the time, full of informal and natural phrases. In those days, the spelling of the word was not standardized, and each playwright spelled words freely. No manuscript signed by Shakespeare survives, but probably he also wrote the manuscript in his own way. As for the stress of each word, it was volatile and sometimes moved to another syllable in order to adjust the tone of the sentence.

Regarding rhyme, Shakespeare used the iambic pentameter which is called Blank Verse (non-rhyming poetry). That is, there were five combinations of weak syllables and strong syllables making one line. Therefore, one line consisted of 10 syllables. For this reason, Shakespeare's word order of the line sometimes changes, moving back and forth.

In Shakespeare's English, the genitive -s is commonly used, although in present-day English, inanimate nouns use of-phrase. In *Julius Caesar* Act III,

"All the world's a stage"

Scene 1, we can notice two successive genitive -*ses*, like "Caesar*s* death*s* houre". With regard to the progressive form, Shakespeare did not make a clear distinction between *be* -*ing* and simple form to describe the progressive form. He just used them differently depending on the context.

As for the imperative, "verb + thou" was generally the basic form at that time. For example, they said, *"Go thou to her"*. But in Shakespeare's English, the meaning of *thou* was also expressed by using *thee* where it should be expected. For example, *"Go thee to her"* (meaning "Go thou to her"). However, this form was the old expression used in Middle English. In addition, the same usage in Modern English without the personal pronouns *thou* or *thee* also appeared in Shakespeare's English.

The word *ought* was originally the past tense of *owe*, but Shakespeare used it to mean *"owe"*. For example, we notice "You ought him a thousand pounds", in *Henry IV Part I*, Act III, Scene 3.

In present-day German, all the nouns use capital letters at the beginning of words, but in Middle English, capital letters are not used. However, in Shakespeare, the capital letters at the beginning of words were used not only in the case of proper nouns, but also when they had a special meaning in their context.

Many verbs, which are now intransitive verbs, were used as transitive verbs in Shakespeare's days. On rare occasions, Shakespeare also used transitive verbs as intransitive verbs.

Shakespeare expressed in the present tense what should be expressed in the past tense, and made the sentence come alive. Shakespeare used the present tense or the past perfect tense to represent what should be used today in the present perfect tense. Shakespeare sometimes used the present tense in sentences that clearly represent the past, in order to express past events more vividly. For example, "He tooke me by the wrist, and held me hard; Then goes he to the length of all his arme;" in *Hamlet* Act II, Scene 1. The definite article *the* was frequently omitted before a noun already defined by another noun, and the personal pronoun *she* was sometimes used instead of *her*. "Yes, you have seen Cassio and she together", in *Othello*, Act IV, Scene 2. Some English expressions might be not necessarily original to Shakespeare, but there is no doubt that the fountain of words magician used those expressions intentionally.

We can see that Shakespeare had many of his works set in Italy or they were deeply related to Italy. For example, *Romeo and Juliet*, *The Merchant of Venice*, *The Comedy of Errors*, *The Tempest*, *Twelfth Night*, *Othello*, *All's Well that Ends Well*, *Julius Caesar*, *Antony and Cleopatra*, *The Winter's Tale*, etc. It is clear that Shakespeare was conscious that Italy was the cultural center of Europe, which was the birthplace of the Renaissance. On the other hand, even though belonging to the Renaissance period in England, Shakespeare's English had little Latin and less Greek. As N. F. Blake said, "Classical Latin was a dead language in which only outstanding literary works had survived; these were regarded as the highest form of human expression. English literature and language could not compete with Latin".[10] But Shakespeare, who paid attention to sounds and rhythms, used Latin only when it sounds more pleasant. He had no interest in the meaning of Latin words, only the sound. Why didn't he want to use Latin or Greek in his play to convey the meaning of the words? Maybe he disliked the trend at the time that Latin and Greek were almighty, and although many of the background of his works adopted Italy, Shakespeare deliberately avoided classical languages. Perhaps it was also because Latin and Greek were not very familiar to the ordinary people at that time. In the theater, the audience could not read anything, and the lines spoken by the actors could be understood by sound alone, which could not always convey its meaning. The plays of Shakespeare's time were more of a play to be heard than a play to be seen. It was a play for the general public. Shakespeare's dialogue, which emphasized the rhythm of sounds, was difficult to understand in a foreign language. It was impossible for English people to enjoy the superb flavor of Shakespeare's play. The process of creating modern words with new meanings by combining one English word with another eventually enriched the English language. Anyone listening could understand the meaning, and it was easy to get an image of the story.

Shakespeare was particular about expressing in English, and continued to challenge himself to express another literary world as much as possible by a simple way. It is said that he created about 1,700 new words. Just as Geoffrey Chaucer wrote *The Canterbury Tales* in English without using French or Italian in the Middle Ages, Shakespeare used English only. As a result, Shakespeare greatly improved the possibilities of the English language and thereafter increased its value as a language of literary expression well accepted all over the world. Shakespeare's English made British literature special. He created many new words and concepts, just as people abused classical words when they needed to express new concepts.

The essence of Shakespeare's literature

Since the modern period, the age of faith has ended and rationalism has risen. The world, which had been under the strong influence of Christianity, was revived to think logically and to study freely, as in the ancient Greek era, and shifted from believing in the teachings of the church to scientific and rational thinking. The obscene expressions of Shakespeare, especially in *Romeo and Juliet*, are clearly a reaction to the oppressed period of the Middle Ages. This is a testament to the fact that sexual expression, which was considered taboo, became freely expressed. The Renaissance period was richer, compared to any other period in English on human liberation and diversity. It is often pointed out that Shakespeare's expressions are sometimes sexual word games (especially *Romeo and Juliet*). Shakespeare also made upper-class women speak obscene language. However, it should be noted that it is a characteristic of the Renaissance era in Europe. Obscene expressions were blatant in some Elizabethan plays, and in some cases, they were set in brothels.[11] Such kind of attitude of Shakespeare was the reflection of the time of that period. But the important thing is that Shakespeare's expression is indirect and cannot be done directly. Some audience may not have understood his intentions. Of course, there were very few religious themes in Shakespeare's dramas. Othello's jealousy, King Lear's anger and disappointment, and Macbeth's ambitions are also full of human touch and would not be appreciated correctly without this context.

Shakespeare coined many new words and idioms. One of them is "love is blind". The term itself has since come into common use by people, but the great talent of Shakespeare is that it carries an important theme of *Romeo and Juliet* itself. It seems that the title, *Romeo and Juliet* was originally not Shakespeare's idea, but somehow used a poem by Arthur Brooke called *The Tragical History of Romeo and Juliet* (1562).[12] However, like *Hamlet*, Shakespeare could skillfully create

SHAKESPEARE

In the Theatre Royal, London

his unique view of the human from the old story that already existed. In *Romeo and Juliet*, in the first scene of Act II, Benvolio, a nephew to the Montague, and a friend to Romeo, says the line, "love is blind". This phrase permeates the whole work like a song motif. *Romeo and Juliet* is a true tragedy that expresses "love is blind" in which Romeo meets Juliet for the first time at a ball and they even promise to get married that day, and Mercutio (friend to Romeo) and Tybalt (nephew to Lady Capulet) are killed in just five days, and finally, Romeo commits suicide after misunderstanding that Juliet died of drinking poison. Juliet, who wakes up from her deep sleep, follows Romeo to suicide. This tragedy is exactly because of "love is blind". Another theme of *Romeo and Juliet* is the prejudice of the two opposing families, the house of Montague and the house of Capulet. Romeo and Juliet, who love each other, are unable to bond because of the bad relationship between the Montague and the Capulet. Their love affair ends with an ironical ending, but in the end, the patriarchs of both families abandoned their hatred, abandoned prejudice, and reconciled. If we pay attention to this part, we can read that love is an irreplaceable concept that can transcend the barriers of different groups or races of culture, common sense, and way of thinking. Love can eliminate evil prejudices, and ultimately unite the world. The meaning of the phrase "love is blind" is that with love, prejudice becomes invisible to our eyes. But while it is certain that prejudice should disappear from this world, it has not been born for absolutely no reason. There will always be prejudice for some reason. It is thought that some kind of trouble arose between the Montague and Capulet families, which could not be resolved, and that they became enemies.

While the ultimate goal remains to completely remove prejudice and to get along with each other, it is dangerous to try to abruptly eliminate the prejudices that originally arose inevitably for each other. What can be interpreted from the phrase "love is blind" is that love is a trigger to abandon prejudice, but at the same time, we sometimes cannot see even the aspect of prejudice that must be firmly faced and resolved. The two, the young boy and girl, who had abandoned prejudice, should not only have made a case for their reconciliation, but also, they should have listened more to the arguments of the prejudiced Montague and Capulet families. I think that's the real tragedy of this story.

Hamlet does not seek for salvation from God

Hamlet is the play 'which may be said to offer the fullest exhibition of Shakespeare's powers.'[13] "To be, or not to be" was pronounced like: [tə] [biː] [ɔr] [nɔt] [tə] [biː]. With this famous line, a long Hamlet's monologue begins, followed by lines of worries about the death of human. However, the content is "To die (is) to sleep" or "in that sleep of death what dreams may come". So it means, "What kind of dreams do we have when we are dead?" And the important thing here is that Hamlet makes no mention of the heaven and hell that Christianity insists. This can be interpreted as an indication of the intention to think for oneself rather than entrusting oneself to Almighty God, answering philosophical questions such as "who one is", "why one was born", and "what one lives for". A glimpse into the genealogy of existentialism in the history of Western philosophy shows that the German philosopher, Nietzsche, at the end of the 19th century said that "Gott starb (God is dead)."[14] And the 20th-century French philosopher, Sartre, proclaimed humanism proudly by claiming that "l'existence précède l'essence (existence precedes essence)."[15] The essence of their argument is that "the meaning or purpose of human life is not something that has been given to us in advance by God, but we make it ourselves." It can be said that the idea in Shakespeare's monologue of Hamlet, written in England in the 17th century, has something in common with the concept of Nietzsche and Sartre that blossomed in the 20th century.

The world of tragedy depicted by Shakespeare is very human. Hamlet does not seek for salvation from God and worries for himself. Hamlet does not rely on God. "To be or not to be" is a symbolic phrase for the suffering of one man himself, in which he does not rely on God for the answer, and the answer must be found by oneself. A man who has lost the Christian spirit eventually comes to a tragic end. They are Othello, King Lear, Macbeth at the mercy of witches, and ambitious Lady Macbeth. They all die tragic deaths. Is there salvation there? Shakespeare warns that human beings have been liberated from oppression and have freedom, and at the same time they will face a tragic end.

The way for modern people to face themselves is having a rational sprit, called reason. Reason objectifies and represents the world, and at the same time it objectifies itself. Modern rationality objectifies the world and measures everything. The important thing is the ability of correct analysis and reflection. By objectifying ourselves internally and in the external world, we must protect ourselves from the risks that befall us. Without this modern way of thinking and scientific spirit, we cannot avoid the human tragedy portrayed by Shakespeare's works.

Shakespeare's English and Modern American English

Since the 17th century, the English language has been stable and established. Supported by a modern spirit of analysis and reflection, English has developed into a more rational language. After that, English has not changed much and has become connected to English used all over the world now. Shakespeare was a fallen child from heaven of the turning point in the history of the English language, and his imagination contributed greatly to enriching English and making its unique linguistic qualities shine through as English transitioned from Middle English to Early Modern English.

William Shakespeare

Shakespeare's works make us well understand the mood of Early Modern English. And we are overwhelmed by its free English expressions. In addition, what is surprising is that some of these minor expressions are now being found in the United States as informal or broken English expressions, and some of them are eventually becoming established as one of the acceptable English expressions again. But I would like to reiterate, some of those expressions were in fact already in use during Shakespeare's time. If we think about Pilgrim Fathers boarded a ship named *Mayflower* and came to the east coast of America in 1620, we could understand that British English in the 17th century has survived in America. Actually, it is said that 17th century British English and modern American English have much in common. Turning nouns into verbs and turning verbs into nouns, and turning pronouns into nouns, can also be seen in the expressions of Shakespeare's time. Even during Early Modern English period, they generally used *who* which is found in today's colloquial expressions, instead of the relative pronoun *whom*. As for pronunciation, it is no coincidence that there is a recent tendency to pronounce a word exactly as it is spelled in American English. It's a phenomenon of "going back to the old days", isn't it?

For intransitive verbs to represent the perfect tense, not "have + past participle" but "be + past participle" also existed in Shakespeare's English. The definite article was omitted by prosody. So, the same word may or may not have *the* before it. If the subject was obvious, it was sometimes omitted. There were various other omissions: verb, article, relative pronoun, and so on.[16] Native speakers would say, "Come and see me." or "Come to see me." But now in American colloquial parlance, they say "Come see me." However, this expression was already in use in Shakespeare's time.

Shakespeare's 37 plays, 154 sonnets, and two narrative poetries (*Venus and Adonis* and *The Rape of Lucrece*) have made great contributions not only in terms of linguistic merit, but also in their content as the literary translation. Shakespeare changed people's way of thinking from the Middle Ages to the modern era, and he also raised the literary world to a level that challenges philosophers. Shakespeare is a model leader for humanism. What is the meaning of Shakespeare's line such as "Fair is foul, and foul is fair" (*Macbeth*, Act I, Scene 1)? This concept is the true essence of Shakespearean world. This irrational way of thinking is a challenge to a philosophy full of a sense of stagnation, which has a discipline that does not allow for consistencies and contradictions. Therefore, Shakespeare proclaims the potential of the literary arts with great prowess. Not only did the linguistic features of Early Modern English influence on present-day English, but also the many characters in his dramas, such as Romeo, Juliet, King Lear, Macbeth, Othello, and Hamlet were ahead of humanism in the Renaissance, in terms of human emotion, affection, and philosophical ideology. And even for modern people in the 21ˢᵗ century, their way of life still continues to influence us because they are what we are. Shakespeare's English world is still eager to see the opportunity to declare its potential.

Tsubouchi Shoyo and Modern novels of Japan

The Theater Museum of Waseda University is a building related to Tsubouchi Shoyo (1859-1935), who taught English literature at Waseda University. He was the first English scholar to translate all of Shakespeare's works into Japanese. He criticized Takizawa Bakin's historical novel *Hakken-den* (1842) because Tsubouchi thought it's just a popular story in which good guys and bad guys fight, and could not be called excellent literature. Bakin (1767-1848) was a great writer of the Edo period (1603-1868) and the first professional writer in Japan to make a living on manuscript fees. Bakin respected great scholars of Japanese literature, such as Hirata Atsutane and Moto-ori Norinaga, and interacted with a painter Watanabe Kazan (the secretary of Tahara Domain) and Katsushika Hokusai, an ukiyo-e artist. His life's work, *Hakken-den* (the legend of the eight young warriors whose names contain the character of a dog) was written under the influence of China's *Suiko-den*. It was undoubtedly a representative work of literature of the Edo period. Bakin wanted to depict a powerful and reliable ideal, only in the world of the novel he wrote.

But Tsubouchi denied this. He only pursued Realism, and argued that it is literature that expresses reality as it is. Strangely enough, afterwards, Natsume Soseki (1867-1916), the pinnacle of Japanese Literature, defended Bakin's idea in his work, *Kusa-makura*, saying, "It is poetry, or painting, that pulls out the troubles of living, from the world of difficulty and reflects the grateful world around you." For Bakin, the novel was an unreal and ideal world. There is no

Tsubouchi Shoyo

doubt that the greatest work of Edo literature is *Hakken-den*. Therefore, Japan's modern novels had to begin with overcoming Bakin. Tsubouchi was well aware of Bakin's greatness, but he believed that Realism was necessary first to Modern Japan. Akutagawa Ryunosuke, representing a short story writer of Japan, wrote a story *Gesaku-zanmai* dealing with Bakin as the main character. Maybe, Ryunosuke also respected Bakin. In fact, Bakin also wrote a voluminous diary. It can be said that Bakin was a realist when he wrote his diary. The diary written by Bakin was full of Realism that Tsubouchi really wanted to get. Now is the time for Japan novelists to write great stories like Takizawa Bakin or William Shakespeare.

The Theater Museum of Waseda University, Tokyo, Japan

8. Dr Johnson's House

The princess thought, that of all sublunary
things, knowledge was the best: she desired
first to learn all sciences, and then purposed
to found a college of learned women,
in which she would preside, that, by
conversing with the old, and educating the
young, she might divide her time between
the acquisition and communication of

Dr. Johnson lived here (1748-59)

wisdom, and raise up for the next age models of prudence, and patterns
of piety. The prince desired a little kingdom, in which he might
administer justice in his own person, and see all the parts of government
with his own eyes; but he could never fix the limits of his dominion, and
was always adding to the number of his subjects.

....

Of these wishes that they had formed they well
knew that none could be obtained.[17]

The History of Rasselas, Prince of Abissinia

Dr. Johnson

Dr Johnson's House (17 Gough Square,
London) is the only surviving townhouse of the
18 houses in the City where Dr. Johnson lived.
He lived in this house from 1748 to 1759, paying
a rent of £30. Here, he compiled *A Dictionary of*

81

Plaque on the wall

the English Language, which was completed in 1755. For this achievement, he received the degree of Master of Arts from the University of Oxford. Later, he was awarded an honorary doctorate by Trinity College Dublin in 1765 and by Oxford University in 1775. Today, there is a commemorative plaque on the front wall of the house.

In the 18th century, Samuel Johnson (1709-84), often called Dr. Johnson, considered a literary magnate in London, was born in Lichfield, Staffordshire, England, where his father ran a small bookstore. His mother was a wise woman who was passionate about educating her children. An illness Johnson suffered as a child that left him deaf in one ear and blind in one eye. Even so, he was famous as an excellent talent from elementary school and was an outstanding honor student. In 1728, a certain patron (philanthropist) paid for his tuition at Pembroke College at Oxford University. So he was able to go to the university. However, his patron stopped paying his tuition halfway through, and Johnson dropped out of college because he could not pay his tuition. When he returned to his hometown, he became a substitute teacher at an elementary school, while also starting to write. At the age of 26, he married Elizabeth Porter (1689-1752), a 46-year-old widow with three stepchildren. With his wife's dowry, Johnson opened a school, but only three pupils were recruited. Two years after getting married, Johnson

Elizabeth Porter

moved to London and became a writer by writing articles to magazines and newspapers. In 1747, at the age of 38, Johnson contracted several publishers to compile an English dictionary, which was published in 1755. When Johnson was 43, Elizabeth died at the age of 63. It was three years before the English dictionary was completed.

James Boswell

In 1759, he wrote his first and last novel (philosophical novella), *Rasselas*. In 1763, he met James Boswell (1740-1795), a native of Scotland, and made Boswell his pupil. Boswell later became known for writing a masterpiece of biographical works, *The Life of Samuel Johnson*. In 1764, Dr. Johnson founded The Club (or Literature Club) with the artist Joshua Reynolds. Members of The Club met once a week (later, once every two weeks) at seven, at the Turk's Head Inn in Gerrand Street, Soho. In 1765, he published "Johnson's edition of Shakespeare", as *The Plays of William Shakespeare* (*Eight Volumes, To which are added Notes by Sam. Johnson*). In his later years, he published *Lives of the English Poets*. In 1769, he was appointed Professor of Classical Literature at the Royal Academy of Arts. He died in December 1784, at the age of 75. Johnson's remains were buried at Westminster Abbey, London.

The template of English-English dictionary

The first English-English dictionary, *A Table Alphabetical,* was published by Robert Cawdrey in 1604. This dictionary was not a general dictionary that contained a wide range of vocabulary, including everyday words. Cawdrey

Statue of Dr. Johnson

defined about 2,500 hard words (loan-words) basically with a single synonym. At any rate, it is worth mentioning that this dictionary was made for the first time for the general public. In 1706, John Kersey's edition of Edward Phillips' *The New World of English Words* appeared. The dictionary is said to be the best of the hard-words dictionaries. It contained about 38,000 words. In 1721, Nathaniel Bailey published his *Universal Etymological English Dictionary*. It contained about 40,000 words. This dictionary had been very popular in many editions. Then Samuel Johnson published *A Dictionary of the English Language* in 1755. He defined or explained over 42,000 words. He introduced as many different meanings of a word as he could. In addition, he made efforts to include as many examples of a single word as possible, and as a result, about 110,000 examples were identified. It is worth noting that this chronological editing method was later used as a template for how to edit English dictionaries. In effect, it was Dr. Johnson who created the form of the English dictionary that exists today. However, his way of explaining was sometimes problematic and quite subjective. For example, *oat* is "a grain, which in England is generally given to horses, but in Scotland supports the people." On the other hand, *castle* is briefly defined as a fortified house,[18] and it's a definition that is still commonly used to describe castles even in castle-related books. The history of this British dictionary compilation eventually completed as *The Oxford English Dictionary* (*OED*) in 1928. It required over 100 years and hundreds of workers to complete. The latest version of *OED* (2015) contains

291,500 major headwords. It contains even those that are no longer used. It also shows when the word was first used and how its meaning changed.

Typical Englishman, Dr. Johnson

Johnson was a tough and hard worker. He says in his book, "Human life is every where a state in which much is to be endured, and little to be enjoyed".[19] His theory of happiness is to accept reality as it is and live a happy life within its limits. This is a concept shared by many British. Dr. Johnson was known as a tea lover and he gulped a lot of tea. He left these words; Tea's proper use is to amuse the idle, and relax the studious...

There is a statue of a cat near Dr Johnson's House. Dr. Johnson loved cats very much and had several of them. But his favorite was a cat named Hodge, which became a statue. Since Hodge loved oysters, an oyster is represented at the foot of the statue of Hodge. At that time, people living in London were able to get a lot of oysters in the Thames, and anyone could eat them. Perhaps Dr. Johnson also liked oysters. By the way, Hodge is on top of a thick book. The message written underneath is "Sir, when a man is tired of London, he is tired of his life; for there is in London all life can afford." The fact that the word *Sir* is at the beginning of a sentence means that actually this is a cat's line. All things are oysters and books, which means that London satisfies appetites and thirst for knowledge. In other words, London satisfies people not only physically but also mentally.

Statue of Hodge

Also nearby is "Ye Olde Chesire Cheese",

one of London's oldest pubs, which Dr. Johnson frequented. Sometimes we see signs in London pubs with "Ye Olde…" to express the meaning of "The Old…". Originally, *The Old* was written as *Þe Olde* in the Middle Ages using the Old English letter thorn (Þ). But when *Þe* was handwritten, because of its resemblance to *Ye*, Þ was often confused with *Y*. Then *Ye* sometimes came to appear when they wanted to express *The* in the second half of the Middle Ages. It is very interesting that it's still used as a pub sign today.

Dr Johnson's House is open to the public.

9. The Sherlock Holmes Museum

When you get off at the Baker Street underground station and go up to the ground level, you will see a statue of Sherlock Holmes standing in front of you. From there, it's a three-minute walk to the Sherlock Holmes Museum. The address is marked on the building as 221B Baker Street. It was set in the novel that Holmes lived there with Dr. Watson, and in 1990, the Sherlock Holmes Museum opened.

The 3-meter-high statue of Holmes

I had seen little of Holmes lately. My marriage had drifted us away from each other. My owns, complete happiness, and the home-centred interests which rise up around the man who first finds himself master of his own establishment, were sufficient to absorb all my attention; while Holmes, who loathed every form of society with his whole Bohemian soul, remained in our lodgings in Baker Street, buried among his old books, and alternating from week to week between cocaine and ambition, the drowsiness of the drug, and the fierce energy of his own keen nature.[20]

'A Scandal in Bohemia'

Sir Arthur Conan Doyle (1859-1930) was born in Edinburgh, Scotland, to an Irish Catholic family. The Doyle family on his father's side was of Norman

Entrance of the museum

descent that emigrated to Ireland from France. His mother's side was also said to have come to Ireland from France. Doyle's grandfather was a prominent caricaturist in London. His uncles were director of the National Gallery of Ireland, painter, illustrator, and others. He graduated from Medical School, University of Edinburgh in 1881. Later, while working as a ship's doctor, a doctor at a local clinic, and a town doctor, he also wrote short stories for a London magazine. He then practiced ophthalmology in London and eventually signed with Strand Magazine, where he was very successful with the Sherlock Holmes series.

Doyle wrote the science fiction novel *The Lost World* (1912), and wrote historical novels, which earned him a certain reputation. But Doyle could not shake off the image of a detective novel writer throughout his life. Doyle received the title of *Sir* from Edward VII in 1902 for his efforts to restore the honor of the British Army in the Boer War.

Many of Doyle's short stories were published in *The Strand Magazine* (1891-1950), a monthly English magazine for the general public to enjoy reading with their family members. Sherlock Holmes series consists of 56 short stories and four long stories, for a total of 60 works (1887-1927). Doyle was a pioneer of detective stories and subsequently, his works became classic, and they are still very popular all over the world. However, what is noteworthy about Doyle's

Holmes stories is that there are many international characters in every story. Dr. Watson, the best friend of Holmes, was a disabled veteran military doctor from Afghanistan. The names of Watson and Mrs. Hudson who lived downstairs and cared for Holmes and Watson, suggest their ancestors came from the Scandinavian Peninsula because of their family names ending in -*son*. King of Bohemia in 'A Scandal in Bohemia' (1891) is the main character of the story, and his former mistress, Irene Adler was born in New Jersey, America, who became an opera singer in Warsaw, Poland. In 'The Boscombe Valley Mystery' (1891), most of the characters involved in the incident were from Australia. In 'The Man with the Twisted Lip' (1891), there is a Chinese villain who runs an opium house in London. Dr. Roylott in 'The Speckled Band' (1892), who killed his step-daughter was once a doctor in India. Henry Wood, a tragic hero in 'The Crooked Man' (1893), was a brave soldier in India. In 'The Greek Interpreter' (1893), main characters were all Greeks. In 'The Final Problem' (1893), Holmes was commissioned by the French government to solve a serious incident, and he last confronted Professor Moriarty at the Swiss waterfall, called the Reichenbach Falls. In 'The Dancing Men' (1903), Elsie, the heroin in trouble came from America to get married to an English gentleman, who was killed by her former American lover. In 'The Six Napoleons' (1904), criminals including Beppo are all Italians. In 'The Abbey Grange' (1904), Lady Mary Brackenstall is a young beautiful woman from Australia. In 'Wisteria Lodge' (1908), there are many Spaniards appearing throughout the whole story. In 'The Problem of Thor Bridge'

Sir Arthur Conan Doyle

(1922), the main character in the story is an American, and his wife was a Brazilian who had killed herself. The stories of Sherlock Holmes are full of international flavor. The Victorian British Empire had many colonies and its territory spread all over the world. It is in the 19ᵗʰ century that the British had already acquired a global sense.

Genealogy of detective novels

Conan Doyle was a pioneering detective novelist. That would be appreciated by everyone. He was followed by Agatha Christie (1890-1976). Detective novels are very popular in Japan as well. To be precise, however, the first detective novel (story) in history was written by an American writer, Edgar Allan Poe (1809-49). It is 'The Murders in the Rue Morgue' published in the United States in 1841. Doyle actually read this work and was undoubtedly strongly influenced by Poe. Another was Charles Dickens' (1812-70) unfinished work, *The Mystery of Edwin Drood* (1870). This work is said to be the first mystery novel in British Literature. Not to mention *Strange Case of Dr Jekyll*

and Mr Hyde (1886) by fellow Scottish writer Robert Louis Stevenson (1850-94).

Doyle began his career as a writer directly in the form of Dickens' newly pioneered genre of detective fiction, but Poe's existence cannot be underestimated. As is expected, I think that the pioneer who created the prototype of the mystery should be Edgar Poe. Poe's talent and genius were not compared to Doyle's, but Poe was a genius writer from another dimension. However, Poe's

Edgar Allan Poe

private life was poor, unstable, drowning in alcohol, and he himself had died a mysterious death at just 40 years old. For this reason, the number of works that can be said to be Poe's detective stories was small (about 5 works). Overall, Poe's work was so unusual in its depicted worldview that it was impossible for the whole family to enjoy the story with the children. Therefore, when we think of detective stories, everyone usually thinks of the adventures of Sherlock Holmes, and we come to recognize that Conan Doyle was the driving force.

In his later years, Doyle had a strong interest in spiritualism and enthusiastically engaged in such lecture activities. This is a gap in the image of Doyle, the writer who portrayed the cold-blooded Sherlock Holmes, which puzzles many Holmes fans (Sherlockian, or Holmesian). However, this may have been out of a desire to emphasize the superiority of the Celtic tribes living in Ireland and Scotland. Don't you think so?

Why mystery stories are popular in the UK

There are many mystery story writers in England. That is, there are so many people who love mystery, and there is a demand for it. Or 19th century Britain was already growing into a modern nation that could accept mystery novels.

First, Britain was getting richer, and literacy increased. People who had never read books before began to read them out of curiosity. They did not want to read philosophical, religious, and esoteric classics. The heart-wrenching storyline was interesting. Detective novels became popular to meet the needs of such readers. Holmes may have been an elite by nature (perhaps upper-middle), but he was portrayed as an eccentric outcast. That must have resonated with readers.

In order to solve a case, the ability to grasp things objectively and the ability to think logically are required. Speaking of novels, there is an image of a work of art that appeals to emotions. The secret of the popularity of mystery in Britain lies in the temperament of the British, who have a deep understanding of art but at the same time have a rationalist aspect. The search for the culprit should not be judged by emotion. It is only after grasping the incident objectively, deducing, narrowing down the culprit by the method of elimination, and solidifying the physical evidence, that, only then, the criminal is arrested. Detective novels can be said to be works that add more logical thinking, reasoning power, and rationality to traditional literary works.

Many point out that the social background of the United Kingdom, that is, the fact that the United Kingdom is a democratic country governed by law, led to the spread of detective novels. Mystery stories cannot grow in a country where the authorities try to solve the case by catching the suspect and forcing him or her to confess by torturing them with insufficient evidence. Detective stories as entertainment are tolerated and accepted if it is a country with a fair police force that goes through the process of scientifical and rational investigation. Because Britain has a society that values human rights, mystery and detective books on the search for criminals have developed.

And one more thing that can be said is that, just as Dickens played the role of admonishing people who no longer went to church, about morality, virtue, the meaning of life, and how people should live sincerely, Doyle wanted to reveal the darkness of the complex and crime-rampant big cities and the minds of corrupt aristocrats in a closed countryside. Doyle wanted to teach his readers the law and educate people about where the crime traps lurked so that they didn't get caught up in rampant crime in their daily life. There must have been a need to raise their awareness of crime prevention.

Britain belongs to the Nordic part of Europe, with dark and long winters. Winter sunsets are rushed, and after 4 p.m., for example, it gets dark around London. The early morning in London in winter is pitch black. When you go outside the house, you can see a thick white mist forming a large round ball around the streetlight. White masses are spread all around and they create a very mysterious atmosphere. As I walked forward on the weird and quiet early morning street, a person walking from the other side suddenly appeared in front of me, and I was horrified. I was keenly aware that this kind of British climate gives birth to detective novels.

The stories describe Holmes and Dr. Watson living here as tenants of Mrs. Hudson.

10. London King's Cross and Harry Potter

King's Cross Station

London King's Cross railway station is the first train station from London to Scotland, that is, the southern terminus of the East Coast Main Line. This station was opened in 1852 by the Great Northern Railway. In the past, if travelers took an overnight train to Scotland from this station, there was a morning tea service the next morning, and besides the teapot and teacup, the staff would bring heaping biscuits on a plate to their compartment. However, King's Cross has now become a tourist attraction where fans gather as a place related to *Harry Potter* written by British author J.K. Rowling (1965-). This station has a Harry Potter-related souvenir shop, named "The Harry Potter Shop at Platform 9 3/4" and is full of people. In addition, there is a place that reproduced "Platform 9 and 3/4" mentioned in the novel, where tourists who want to take a commemorative photo form a long line and wait for their turn.

'I just take the train from platform nine and three-quarters at eleven o'clock,' he read.

His aunt and uncle stared.

'Platform what?'

'Nine and three-quarters.'

'Don't talk rubbish,' said Uncle Vernon, 'there is no platform nine and three- quarters.'

'It's on my ticket.'[21]

What is the secret of the popularity of the Harry Potter series? There are seven fantasy novels in the series, from *Harry Potter and the Philosopher's Stone* to *Harry Potter and the Deathly Hallows*. The contents of each work are very attractive and rich in contrast, which does not bore the readers. The contrast between children and adults, the rich and the poor, logical and emotional, positive and negative, and the magical world and the real world: these contrasts are indeed, the result of the British sense of balance. Of course, the plot is very interesting. However, if you read the work carefully, you can receive author's another message. For example, when Harry enrolls in a wizarding school named Hogwarts, he is to be divided into four pairs: Gryffindor, Hufflepuff, Ravenclaw, and Slytherin.

'Potter, Harry!'

As Harry stepped forward, whispers suddenly broke out like little hissing fires all over the hall.

'*Potter*, did she say?'

'*The* Harry Potter?'

The last thing Harry saw before the hat dropped over his eyes was the Hall full of people craning to get a good look at him. Next second he was looking at the black inside of the hat. He waited.

'Hmm,' said a small voice in in his ear. 'Difficult. Very difficult. Plenty of courage, I see. Not a bad mind, either. There's talent, oh my goodness, yes-and a nice thirst to prove yourself, now that's interesting...

Enjoying taking photos   Harry Potter Shop

So where shall I put you?'[22]

Harry Potter and Philosopher's Stone

At this time, Harry was judged by the Hogwarts Sorting Hat to be the predisposition to go to a class called Gryffindor, which students are brave-minded and reformist, and also to a class called Slytherin, which students are ambitious, discriminatory, conservative in keeping with old traditions, and do not choose any means for their enemies. The Hat said that if Harry goes to Slytherin, his talent

will blossom. But Harry wanted to go to Gryffindor. So, the Hat respected Harry's will and sent him to Gryffindor. What this episode tells us is that the will of the person to become what kind of person he wants to be, is more important than the person's nature or qualities. In the Harry Potter series, characters with various personalities such as good guys and bad guys appear, but they are not born good or bad, but often choose that path of their own volition under the guidance of a menter.

J.K. Rowling said with more powerful words in her 2008 graduation speech at Harvard University in the United States. When she chose a university course, she didn't follow her parents' advice. She got behind the wheel of the car called her life, and moved forward. She wanted to control her life on her own.

> … I do not blame my parents for their point of view. There is an expiry date on blaming your parents for steering you in the wrong direction; the moment you are old enough to take the wheel, responsibility lies with you.[23]

British women writers, standing out

If we look around the history of British literature, it can be said that women writers stand out : Jane Austen is famous for her work *Pride and Prejudice*. Mary Shelley is famous for the Gothic novel *Frankenstein*. Charlotte Brontë is famous for *Jane Eyre*. Emily Brontë is famous for *Wuthering Heights*. Anne Brontë is famous for *Agnes Grey* and *The Tenant of Wildfell Hall* (1848). George Eliot is famous for *Silas Marner* and *Middlemarch* (1872). Ouida is famous for *A Dog of Flanders*, especially in Japan. Agatha Christie is world famous for *Murder on the Orient Express* (1934) and *And Then There Were None* (1939). Dodie Smith (1896-1990) wrote *The Hundred and One Dalmatians* (1956). Anne Fine (1947-) is famous for *Madame Doubtfire* (1987), which was made into a movie as *Mrs. Doubtfire* in the USA in 1993 and is now one of the staples of musicals in London. Then, the most successful female writer, J.K. Rowling (1965-) appeared in 1997.

Jane Austen (1775-1817) was the first female novelist in England. Her

① Jane Austen, ② Mary Shelley, ③ Charlotte Brontë, ④ Emily (right) and Anne (left) Brontë,
⑤ George Eliot, ⑥ Ouida

father, George Austen graduated from the University of Oxford, and became a parish rector in the county of Hampshire, southern England. Austen's masterpiece is *Pride and Prejudice* (1813). In the story, Austen just depicted ordinary and innocent events in everyday life with people in a middle-class family in the countryside of England. Characters are conservative, not to make political or social statements, and don't say the slightest hint of social advancement of women. The author's argument is that a woman's happiness is to marry a rich and gentle person. But the characters are realistic and Austen is skillful at depicting the psychological description of young heroines. Of course, the heroin she portrayed was not a woman who would be at the mercy of men, but an intelligent woman who spoke out of her opinions. Austen's fame came after her death.

Mary Shelley (1797-1851) is considered a pioneer of science fiction, but her grotesque novel world is full of fear, despair and cruelty. Her father was the political philosopher, William Godwin and her husband was the Romantic poet, Percy Shelley. Mary published the first edition of *Frankenstein* anonymously in 1818.

Charlotte Brontë (1816-54) was the third of the six children (five daughters and a son). She published *Jane Eyre* in 1847 under the male name *Currer Bell*. The initials of the pen-name C.B. are the same initials as her name Charlotte *Brontë*. Brontë was not conservative and had a very radical personality. She portrayed strong-willed young girls, economically independent women, and women standing up to society in her novels. She was the eldest of three Brontë sisters: other two sisters are Emily Brontë (1818-48), whose masterpiece is *Wuthering Heights* (1847), and Anne Brontë (1820-49), whose masterpiece is *Agnes Grey* (1847). Brontë sisters' father was an Irish Anglican rector in Yorkshire, and their mother was weak and died at the age of 38. When Charlotte was eight years old, four of her five daughters were sent to a boarding school, but due to the poor dormitory life, two of them died from

J.K. Rowling

99

illness. Later, Charlotte went to school again to become a governess. Charlotte's masterpiece, *Jane Eyre*, is a powerful story about a young woman who seeks financial independence working as a governess. *Jane Eyre* is a story about a rebellious orphan girl with a sense of gender equality, who grows up and eventually falls in love with Mr. Rochester, the owner of the manor house where she lives as a governess. Charlotte Brontë wanted to depict the world of love marriage that is not bound by social status. She also wanted to show a new image of a woman, who is strong, intelligent, and independent. Jane Eyre, the heroine of the story is a woman who can control her own life. Her way of life aroused a great response at the time.

George Eliot (1819-80), whose real name was Mary Ann(e), showed the world where good perishes and evil flourishes in her books. That was a typical Victorian novel pattern to make readers find that working hard and living with integrity would lead to success in life. *Silas Marner : The Weaver of Raveloe* (1861) is a clear example of this theme. The summary of this story is as follows: Silas Marner, a weaver, is said to have stolen money, abandoned by the woman he promised to marry, and forced to flee the town Lantern Yard where he lived. In fact, he did not steal anything. Silas moves to a small village named Raveloe, where he continues to work steadily as a weaver and saves money. One day, however, all of his gold coins were stolen. Then, on New Year's Eve, a baby girl who was only two years old wanders into Silas' house. Her mother collapsed and died in the snow. Silas considers the girl to be his treasure given by God and raises her with great care. Eventually, the child, Eppie (his adopted daughter) grows up and falls in love with a good local young man Aaron Winthrop and marries him. The stolen gold coins are also officially returned to Silas, who lives happily with close friends and new family. I'm sure this is a typical Victorian bildungsroman, comparable to Dickens' works.

Ouida (1839-1908) whose father was French and mother was English, was born at Bury St Edmunds in Suffolk, England. *Ouida* was the pseudonym (pen name), and her real name was Marie Louise de la Ramée. Known for her love of dogs, she lived with many dogs in her later years. She was also enthusiastic about animal welfare activities. Her novel *A Dog of Flanders* (1872) was animated in Japan and is a fairly famous work, but its negative ending was not particularly popular in the United States, and it was rewritten to end with a happy ending. It is not popular even in Belgium, where this work is set, and the locals do not know the story.

Agatha Christie (Dame Agatha Mary Clarissa Christie, Lady Mallowan, 1890-1976) was an international bestselling author of detective novels. She was born in Devon, southwest England, to an American father and an English mother, but her father went bankrupt and died of illness. In parallel with her own marriage to a military man, divorce, and remarriage with a younger archaeologist, Sir Max Mallowan, she wrote 66 detective novels and 14 short stories. She was made a Dame by Queen Elizabeth for her contributions to literature. After the Bible and Shakespeare's works, her books (more than two billion copies) were said to be read all over the world.

After all, there is a reason why there are so many female writers in the UK. First of all, in Britain, where Shakespeare was born, literature is a national specialty, and the denominator is probably larger than in other countries. In a country where individualism has developed, there are many personal opinions and ideas. Sometimes, a new story is born, and sometimes it turns into a big story. The profession of writer appeared in England during the 18th and 19th centuries. In the United Kingdom, a country of class society, children took over their father's occupation, so there are basically few opportunities to work in another profession that was different from that of the parents. However, at that time, the profession of writer, which was born as a new industry, was not hereditary. It was a growing industry and there were many vacancies. Wasn't there a rush of women there? With such a social background, the writer industry may have gained popularity at the time as a job that women with literary talents who wanted to become economically independent could do. It continues to this day.

J.K. Rowling's Success Story

The profile of J.K. Rowling, Britain's most famous and most money-making female writer today, implied that she would become a popular writer because her life itself is a drama and a success story. Rowling was born in 1965 in Yate, Gloucestershire, southwest England. Her father was an engineer, and her mother passed away in 1990 after 10 years of serious illness. She had loved reading and writing novels since she was a child. She often read Jane Austen, and others. She studied French and classics at the University of Exeter. While still a student, she studied abroad in Paris for one year. After graduating from university, she worked as a secretary in London and continued to write novels in cafes. The first Harry Potter book was also written at the Elephant House, a cafe in Edinburgh, Scotland. She lived with a man she had met at a bar, became pregnant, had a miscarriage, then got married, gave birth to her first daughter, but divorced four months later. Until the age of 27, she received welfare and housing allowance, and in poverty she wrote novels. Holding her baby daughter, Rowling became depressed at the age of 29 and thought of suicide. She received a grant from the Scottish Department of Education and Industry, and obtained a teaching license. At the age of 30, she completed the manuscript of *Harry Potter*. In 1997, *Harry*

Potter and the Philosopher's Stone was published. The book was translated into 78 languages and sold 600 million copies worldwide. The film starring Daniel Radcliffe (1989-) was a huge success, turned into a stage drama, and Rowling became an unprecedented bestselling author (the most paid author in history). She is now remarried to a doctor and gave birth to two children, a boy and a girl.

Harry Potter's Britain

Places associated with Harry Potter are now one of the highlights of British tourism. Next to King's Cross is St Pancras International Station, opened in 1868. The station including station hotel is a great Neo-Gothic building in red brick, reminiscent of a medieval castle. This station was used in the film, *Harry Potter and the Chamber of Secrets* (2002), as King's Cross. The "Millennium Bridge" over the River Thames was also a film setting for the Harry Potter series. If you leave London, the setting for the shooting of Harry Potter movies spread to various parts of Britain such as Oxford University and Alnwick Castle in Northumberland, England. At the same time, people who visit Britain as a result of *Harry Potter* are naturally dragged into the charm of England and Scotland as if they were enchanted.

St Pancras International Station

103

11. Soseki and London

Natsume Soseki (1867-1916) was a great novelist in modern Japan. His portrait appeared on the front of Japanese 1,000 yen note in 1984. When he was 33 years old, Soseki, a high school English teacher in Kyushu, was ordered to go to England as a scholarship student sponsored by the Japanese Government. On the 28th of October,

Natsume Soseki

Meiji 33 (1900), he arrived in London and started to study English Literature until December 1902. Nervous Soseki changed boarding houses (lodgings) five times during his two years in London. The first was at 76 Gower Street, near the British Museum and the University of London, but the rent was so high that he left in two weeks. The second boarding house was a two-story brick building at 85 Priory Road, a residential area in the West Hampstead. But Soseki stopped staying in six weeks because he could not get used to the atmosphere of the family who were immigrants from Germany. The third was at 6 Flodden Road, but the building was shabby and the owner was an engineer whom Soseki didn't get along with because they didn't get any topic across. Then Soseki thought about moving his boarding house again and checked a newspaper advertisement, but couldn't find any good rooms. At that time, the owner had a financial crisis and had to move to the southern outskirts of London, and Soseki moved with them. The fourth boarding house was a new house at 5 Stella Road, but too far from the center of London. Soseki decided to ask a newspaper company in London to put an advertisement asking for a boarding house. Then he found the house of the Miss Leale sisters (Priscilla and Elizabeth) at 81The Chase. He spent one and a half of his two-year study abroad in London there. The sisters were educated in literature and even had knowledge of French. Soseki finally found an educated family where he could discuss literature. The nearby Battersea Park is two kilometers away, but Soseki seems to have often gone out to the park on a bicycle that he started to change his mind.

Soseki's real name is Kinnosuke. He was born on February 9, 1867 in Ushigome, Edo (present-day Kikui-cho, Shinjuku-ku, Tokyo). His father was *Na-nushi*, the representative of the area they lived. Soon after his birth, Soseki was placed in foster care by the owner of an antique store (or greengrocer). He was returned to his parents' house, but one year later, he was adopted by the Shiobara

The house that Soseki chose as his final lodgings (far right side)

81 The Chase

family. Due to the divorce of his adoptive parents, he was returned to his birthplace at the age of 9, but he was Shiobara Kinnosuke on the family register. When he was 14, he lost his real mother. It was when he was 21 years old that he officially returned to Natsume Kinnosuke. In 1893, he graduated from Tokyo Imperial University (majoring in English Literature) and became an English teacher at *Koto-Shihan*, the national teacher training school in Tokyo at the age of 26.

In 1895, Soseki went to Matsuyama in Ehime Prefecture, to become a junior high school English teacher. The following year, he became an English teacher at Dai-go (the Fifth) High School located in Kumamoto Prefecture, Kyushu. He married Nakane Kyoko (1877-1963), the daughter of a high-ranking government official. In 1900, he was ordered to study English Language (or English Teaching Methods) in England by the Ministry of Education.

Because of the increase in the budget due to the reparations obtained from the victory in the Sino-Japanese War (1894-95), the number of students sent abroad, doubled from 20 to 39.

In the past, only the students in the fields of engineering, medicine, and social sciences were allowed to study abroad. For example, Mori Ogai (1862-1922), who later became a great novelist in Japan, had studied medicine in Germany for four years from 1884 to 1888. Now, language teachers were also given the opportunity to study abroad in order to improve their language skills. As a result, it was decided to send two students to England (Soseki and Kanda

Naibu) and two to Germany (Fujishiro Teisuke and Yamaguchi Kotaro). In the same year, a great composer, Taki Rentaro (1879-1903), was also sent to Germany to study music.

By the way, who recommended Soseki as a scholarship student? The person was directly the principal of the Blue plaque

school where Soseki worked. But it is easy to imagine that he was recommended by his father-in-law, who wanted to promote his son-in law's social position. Actually, Soseki himself had no desire to study abroad. Soseki's interest was not in English teaching methods nor English language, but in English Literature. So, he had to confirm this fact with the person in charge of studying abroad at the Ministry of Education, immediately after receiving the decree. The person in charge replied, "Since it is a public stance, you do not stick to the distinction between language and literature."

During the 40-day voyage, the scholarship students who accompanied Soseki were Fujishiro Teisuke and Haga Yaichi (who went to Germany to study literary history). After arriving at the port of Genova via Naples in Italy, Soseki headed overland to Paris, from which he took the train and ship to London Victoria Station. At first, Soseki considered studying at Cambridge University, but he gave up due to the lack of well-organized English Literature courses and the high cost of tuition, so he chose the University of London. He then audited the newly formed English Literature class at University College London. However, he was not interested in the content of the class (dealing with medieval English literature) and could not get used to the atmosphere of the class. So, he was introduced to

Battersea Park

Shakespeare scholar, William Graig, who was from Ireland, by a professor at the University of London. Soseki went to Graig's boarding house for a while after that, and took private lessons.

While studying abroad, Soseki bought a huge number of books and spent his days reading. Especially, he liked Romantic poetry such as Wordsworth, Shelley, and Keats. It is worth mentioning that Soseki purchased over 500 books during his stay in London. While in the UK, he often got sick, and although he studied in his room almost all day, the report to the Ministry of Education that he had to submit was blank. One of acquaintances was worried about Soseki's condition, visited Soseki's lodging, and sent a telegram to Japan saying Soseki was mentally diseased. Then Soseki was ordered to return to Japan. He left London in December 1902 and returned to Japan in January of the following year.

Incidentally, while Soseki was in London, Queen Victoria died (January 22, 1901), and her funeral was held on February 2. Soseki went out to observe the funeral procession. It marked the beginning of a new Edwardian era. It is also noteworthy that the Anglo-Japanese Alliance was concluded on January 30, 1902. In other words, Britain was full of pro-Japan people at that time. Naturally, Soseki would have been treated favorably by the British. Nevertheless, Soseki felt lonely, isolated and suffered a nervous breakdown during his stay in London. It must have been due to his weak and delicate personality.

Upon returning to Japan, Soseki became a lecturer at Dai-ichi (The First)

High School and Tokyo Imperial University, but his students' reputation was not good. Soseki had a nervous breakdown again, and the number of cancellations of his lectures and substitutions for his lectures increased. It is said that during the lecture, the dog barked and it was too noisy for him to give the lecture. While separated from his wife for two months, in January 1905 (at the age of 38), 'I am a Cat' was published as a short story in the haiku magazine, *Hototogisu*, and the short story 'Tower of London' was also published in the literary magazine, *Imperial Literature*, in the same year. Thereafter, 'I am a Cat' was serialized intermittently and was well received. Soseki decided to become a professional writer, and his 'Cat' was later published as Soseki's first novel.

After that, Soseki wrote *Botchan* (in the same magazine *Hototogisu*). In 1907 (at the age of 40), he resigned his university job and signed a contract with the Asahi Shimbun, a newspaper company, to write serialized novels. *Gubijinso*, *Kohu* (Miner), *Yume-juya*, *Sanshiro*, *Sorekara*, *Mon* (Gate), *Higan-sugimade*, *Ko-jin*, etc. were serialized in newspapers, and later these were released as a book by many publishers. In 1914 (age 47), his masterpiece *Kokoro* (Heart) was serialized in the Asahi from April to August, and in November he gave a lecture on 'My Individualism' at Gakushu-in (school). In 1915, he serialized *Inside the Glass Door* and *Michikusa* in the Asahi, and in May 1916, he started to write *Light and Dark*. However, on December 9 of the same year, he died at home due to internal bleeding (aged 49 years and 10 months). For a long time, Soseki had been suffering from a serious stomach ulcer.

When Soseki became famous as a writer, his adoptive father, Mr. Shiobara, asked him for money. In addition, not only some heartless pupils, but also his father-in-law, Mr. Nakane asked him for money as well. The reason why Soseki was able to return to his parents' house was not because of his family's affection for him but because of his excellent grades at school. Soseki despised and resented Natsume Family. On the other hand, from the perspective of his wife, he had a strong sense of duty in everything; he was very helpful to everyone. Throughout his life, Soseki was pessimistic and always had doubts about studying English. Soseki even felt uncomfortable learning about the literature through English. In his heart, there was a dislike of the self-promotion principle or the rising-career principle that flourished in the Meiji era. He also constantly suffered from stomach ulcers, pulmonary tuberculosis, extreme nervous breakdowns, and so on.

The London Soseki Museum was established in 1984, opposite Soseki's last boarding house (81 The Chase). Recently, the number of visitors continued to decrease year by year. Missed by many Soseki fans, the museum was closed in 2016. It reopened in a new location in southeast England in 2019, but again it was unfortunately closed due to Covid-19.

Conversation with Prof. Deguchi Yasuo

Soseki was an anti-authority English literary scholar, who did not drink alcohol, liked tea, liked watercolor painting, and did not wish for a successful career or the reputation of society. In addition, Soseki liked to read the poems of Wordsworth and Keats. This is very similar to my graduate school supervisor, Professor Deguchi Yasuo

Mori Ogai

Goethe

(1929-2019), a scholar of English Literature at Waseda University in Tokyo.

Prof. Deguchi loved Soseki very much and had written many books about Soseki's studying abroad experience in London. In 1984, as part of the opening ceremony of the Soseki Museum, he gave a lecture titled "Natsume Soseki in London" at the Park Lane Hotel near Hyde Park. The opening ceremony was also attended by Kaifu Toshiki (1931-2022) and Obuchi Keizo (1937-2000), who were members of the House of Representatives at the time (both later became Prime Ministers of Japan). Prof. Deguchi became the honorary director of the Soseki Museum. I have heard that in those days, the current Emperor of Japan was studying at Oxford University and His Majesty, who was the Crown Prince at the time, once visited the Soseki Museum.

One day, I told my master, "I like and respect Mori Ogai more than Soseki because I think Ogai had all the literary talent and linguistic ability", and he replied like this, "Mr. Nishino, when you get a little older, you will understand how good Soseki is." Now I'm old enough, but I'm still trying to find the answer. But, one thing that came to my mind is Soseki's sense of distrust of the modern state. Soseki always had doubts about the idea of a way of life in which career advancement was the most important one. He refused a doctorate in literature when offered by the Ministry of Education. Many of his novels, such as *Sanshiro*, deal with the theme of a local genius entering a prestigious Dai-ichi High School and questioning his rise to prominence in society.

When I was talking about this with my second son, Yasumasa, who had just returned to Japan from England, he asked me the following question.

"Daddy, by the way, when did Soseki decide to become a writer?"

Thinking about it again, it is clear that Soseki began writing novels after studying abroad. I wonder who motivated him to do that. Was Soseki's model

Dickens? Conan Doyle was already active at the time. Both Dickens and Doyle submitted their works to magazines, serialized them, and published them as a book. Maybe, Soseki learned about this style while in England. Just like Ogai learned from Goethe (1749-1832) and tried to connect with the state authorities, Soseki, getting to know the British writers, signed a contract with a newspaper company in Tokyo. Soseki happened to study abroad in England, which was one of the first in the world to succeed in the Industrial Revolution, where the middle class began to empower in society, and where professional writers could write and make a living without the patrons of aristocrats or other state powers. Thanks to the contribution of Soseki, who started the newspaper serialization, later the position of professional writers may have established in Japan. Come to think of it, Prof. Deguchi used to tell me, "Mr. Nishino, the first thing is getting your work published in a magazine. Then ask the editor to serialize it. When you accumulate it, make it into a book."

In order to revive the Natsume family, Soseki was asked to rise to prominence, forced to study English, and actually hated English. When he was 33 years old, Soseki was ordered to study abroad in England even though he did not want to. Suffered from a nervous breakdown, returned to Japan without producing results, not good at teaching English at university, and worrying about becoming a researcher of English Literature, Soseki became a writer. However, in the general public, there was a surprise that a person who graduated from Imperial University and studied in the UK, became a lecturer at Imperial University, resigned from his job at the university, and joined a newspaper. The common people wanted to know what the super elite of Tokyo Imperial University thought on a daily basis, and they really wanted to read what he wrote. So, the newspaper sold well, and Soseki became very popular.

"Literature is essentially 'sad music of humanity'", Prof. Deguchi often admonished me, quoting Wordsworth. I think that literature is essentially the manifestation of the soul of the loser. Ogai, who had excellent language skills, wrote many medical papers, and obtained a doctorate, became mainstream as a military doctor, and at the same time reigned in the world of Japanese literature. Ogai had the highest career as a military doctor in Japan, and was an outstanding historical novelist with deep connections with the powerful people of the state. On the other hand, even after becoming famous, Soseki was constantly devoted to being a private citizen, living a humble life surrounded by disciples, and worried about the modern Japan of self-advancement. Soseki was probably more correct and preferred as a literary figure rather than Ogai, who had outstanding ability and achieved great success in his life.

A statue of Thomas Carlyle stands close to the house where Carlyle lived. Soseki once visited the house during his stay in London.

12. Royal Parks in London

Serpentine Bridge between Kensington Gardens and Hyde Park

There are many beautiful parks in London. Some of them are royal parks with vast green spaces. London is one of the greenest cities in the world. There are lawns, large ponds with swans and ducks, flower beds with seasonal flowers, Italian and English gardens, families with children taking a stroll, and many men and women sunbathing in fine weather. Sometimes you can see squirrels on their way up the trees. St James's Park is London's oldest royal park and borders Buckingham Palace and St James's Palace. St James's Park Lake, where ducks float and swim, is also very beautiful. However, considering the size of each park, London's iconic parks or the most representative parks in London are Hyde Park, Kensington Gardens, and Regent's Park.

An old man, the Duke of Wellington, strolling through Hyde Park

Hyde Park was once a fiefdom of Westminster Abbey. But during Henry VIII, the King took the land (1536), and many deer were left to roam free as a royal hunting ground. It is said that the park's name comes from the Manor of Hyde. The hyde (hide) was an English unit of land measurement (60-120 acres). It was opened to the public in the 17th century. It appears to be integrated with Kensington Gardens, but actually it is divided in half by Serpentine Lake, which is an artificial pond created by damming the River Westbourne, at the suggestion of Queen Caroline of George II. If you go around these two parks, it is about 8 kilometers long. In 1851, it became the site of the Great Exhibition. At that time, the Crystal Palace was built and became the main venue. At the eastern end of Hyde Park is the Hyde Park Corner Entrance, but across the street is the Statue of the Duke of Wellington. The Wellington Arch is nearby, and the Duke of Wellington's townhouse was located nearby. The house, called Apsley House, is now the Wellington Museum and houses a collection of paintings collected by the first Duke of Wellington.

Arthur Wellesley (1769-1852), 1st Duke of Wellington, known as the Duke of Wellington, was born in Dublin, as the third son of an Anglo-Irish noble family. He left Eton College and graduated from the Military Academy in France. He then joined the British Army. After a number of military careers, he ran for the House of Commons from the Tory party and was elected, becoming a statesman. In 1807, he joined the cabinet as Chief Secretary for Ireland. However, the following year, when the war against France began, he led the

Statue of Wellington

British Army to the continent as commander, and won a series of battles against the French Army one after another. For his achievements, he was made Earl of Wellington in the county of Somerset in 1812, and became a nobleman. In 1814, he became Duke of Wellington, and the following year, in 1815, he fought and defeated Napoleon's army at Waterloo, Belgium, in order to defeat the resurgent Napoleon. After fleeing to Paris, Napoleon finally surrendered completely (Battle of Waterloo, Bataille de Waterloo). The Duke of Wellington later served as Prime Minister twice, in 1828-30 and 1834-35, then as Foreign Secretary, and then as Commander-in-Chief of the British Army until his death. When he died in 1852 at the age of 83, the funeral took place at St Paul's Cathedral. In his later years, he often walked around Hyde Park to keep up his strength.

The cover photo of the Beatles album, *Beatles For Sale*, was taken in Hyde Park in the fall of 1964. Other famous attractions include Speakers'

Rotten Row

Hyde Park Rose Garden

Corner, Winter Wonderland, and Rotten Row (route du roi, the King's Road), which remains as a broad track for horses to connect St James's Palace and Kensington Palace.

Peter Pan in Kensington Gardens

The area including Kensington Palace was originally the site of Nottingham Cottage. In 1689, the property was purchased by William III, who ordered to expand the house (now Kensington Palace). Kensington Gardens is one of the royal parks, and is located on the west side of Hyde Park. There is also the 52.5-meter-high Albert Memorial (Albert's statue is 4.2 meters high) in the park, and outside the park is the oval, domed red brick Royal Albert Hall of Arts and Sciences. The hall was built in 1871 to commemorate Queen Victoria's husband, Prince Albert (1819-61), and since then, it has been a multi-purpose hall where concerts and various events are held.

From the Albert Memorial in Kensington Gardens, heading north towards the Lancaster Gate (tube station) or to the Italian Gardens in the park, you will find a statue of Peter Pan, erected in 1912 near Serpentine Lake. There is a children's playground around there. The quote is from the beginning of *Peter Pan in Kensington Gardens*.

The Albert Memorial

You must see for yourselves that it will be difficult to follow Peter Pan's adventures unless you are familiar with the Kensington Gardens. They are in London, where the King lives, and I used to take David there nearly every day unless he was looking decidedly flushed.[24]

Peter Pan in Kensington Gardens

Sir James Matthew Barrie (1860-1937), author of the Peter Pan series, lived near the park during his lifetime. In 1902, when he wrote *The Little White Bird*, he made the first appearance of Peter Pan in it, and in 1904, he published the play, *Peter Pan; or, the Boy Who Wouldn't Grow Up* (three acts), which was a great success. In 1906, he published the children's book *Peter Pan in Kensington Gardens*, in 1911, he published the novel *Peter (Pan) and Wendy*, and in 1928, the play *Peter Pan* (five acts).

Born in Scotland, Barrie graduated from the University of Edinburgh and worked for a newspaper while writing for magazines, and eventually he became a writer. In Kensington Gardens, he met Llewellyn Davies' five sons, who inspired him to write *Peter Pan*. Peter Pan is said to be the eldest son of the family, George (1893-1915). The model for the Peter Pan statue erected in the park is said to be the fourth son, Michael (1900-21). After the death of the couple (Arthur and Sylvia), Barrie had been raising

J. M. Barrie

Peter Pan Statue

their children and supporting them financially. Barrie became Rector of the University of St Andrews in 1919, and he served as Chancellor of the University of Edinburgh from 1930 to 1937.

Barrie was 161 cm tall, and would have been small for an Englishman. He might have been a naïve person who continued to have the heart of a child even as an adult. In fact, he had an older brother who was eight years older than him, but he died in an accident when he was 14 years old. His mother, who adored her dead son, used to say things like that the deceased boy would forever remain a boy and never grow up, but would always be by her side. It could be said that such an experience created a boy named Peter Pan who did not grow up. Or, just as Lewis Carroll gave birth to *Alice's Adventures in Wonderland* (1865) from his interactions with a little girl Alice in Oxford, Barrie met boys in Kensington Gardens and gave birth to *Peter Pan*.

Regent's Park

The Regent's Park is one of the royal parks in north-west London and is a vast park full of nature. The park includes the Marylebone Green Playground, Triton and Dryads Fountain, Japanese Garden Island floating on the pond, Queen Mary's Rose Gardens with 400 kinds of roses, St John's Lodge Garden, The Royal Parks, and the expansive Boating Lake. Near the northern end of the park, a zoo was opened in 1827 for the Zoological Society of London. The zoo (London Zoo) opened to the public in 1828. The land, originally owned by Barking Abbey, was

George IV

Walking through the vast park

taken by Henry VIII and became the property of the royal family, where deer were kept for the royal hunting ground. In 1811, George (1762-1830, later George IV) became Prince Regent to support his father, King George III (r. 1760-1820), who suffered from mental illness. George, the Prince Regent, began remodeling the park, including the development of terraced houses, and the name of the park was changed to Regent's Park, which was opened to the public the following year in 1812. Regent Street (a major shopping street in London) was created to connect Regent's Park with Carlton House near St James's Park. When the Prince Regent became King George IV, he wanted a more magnificent palace than his mansion, Carlton House. Then King George converted Buckingham House into Buckingham Palace and moved there. Carlton House was demolished and a beautiful white Carlton House Terrace was built.

In the 21st century, people's health consciousness has improved, and sports facilities have been expanded and developed in the park. The U.S. ambassador's residence, Winfield House, is located in the park. The building is in Neo-Georgian town-house style. In 2009, President Obama and the first lady, Michelle Obama, arrived for the G 20 Summit in London, and they stayed at the historic house. In Walt Disney's animated film, *One Hundred and One Dalmatians*, the park where Pongo and his owner Roger go for a walk is set in the Regent's Park.

In the park, there is Regent's University London, one of the few private universities in the UK. Founded in 1984, it also has a language school and accepts many international students. By the way, if we look at the number of universities around the world, the USA ranks first with about 2,600 universities. Japan ranks second with about 790 universities, South Korea ranks third with about more than 400 universities, Germany ranks fourth with 370 universities, the UK ranks fifth with about 170 universities, and France ranks sixth with 94 universities. In terms of the number of university students, China is in first place, India is in second place, and the USA is in third place. Japan ranks ninth. In developed countries, the declining birthrate and aging population have become a serious social problem. How to accept international students from all over the world is the key to the survival of universities, or how to get young people around the world interested in Japan and come to Japan will be the key to the economic revival of Japan.

Wordsworth's view of nature

London is not only an entertainment and shopping district, but also a business and political center. Those who live there are workers, merchants, immigrants, the unemployed, and so on. Politicians, officials, office workers, and trading company workers go to work there during the day, and luxury hotels and guesthouses are filled with tourists from all over the world. Traffic is congested and petty crimes are common. In London, which can be called a filthy and miscellaneous stateless zone, there are many beautiful parks reminiscent of the countryside near London. How quiet and calm these parks

A squirrel in the park

121

Triton and Dryads Fountain

are, creating green aesthetic spaces. These parks are the spiritual centers and the origin of vitality for the people living and working in London. Green is essential for the restoration of humanity. Although Britain is disgracefully called the weakened old power, Britain is still alive and well, not perishing, and worth existing. Walking through London's vast, green royal parks, I realize the underlying power of Britain.

> Books! 'tis a dull and endless strife:
> Come, hear the woodland linnet,
> How sweet his music! On my life,
> There's more of wisdom in it.
>
> And hark! how blithe the throstle sings!
> He, too, is no mean preacher:
> Come forth into the light of things,
> Let Nature be your Teacher.[25]

'The Tables Turned'

The advent of the Romantic poet Wordsworth dramatically changed the British sense of beauty towards nature. It's different from the rationalist French who think nature is imperfect or the Americans who think nature is something that man can conquer. It is somewhat similar to that of Japanese people.

Looking at the social background of Britain when Wordsworth was born, first of all, the Industrial Revolution in the 18th century can be cited as a major historical event. The world changed a lot since then. Science and technology moved

The Japanese Garden Island in Regant's Park

the world. Sir Richard Arkwright invented the water frame spinning machine (1771). James Watt built the first efficient steam engine (1776). The first typewriter (1851), telephone (1875), electric light bulb (1878), sewing machine (1886), and camera (1888) were invented in Britain. Military weapons progressed, and overseas explorations were further expanded. People in Britain abandoned the countryside and came to the cities to work as laborers. Their way of thinking became utilitarian, and they began to think based on the concept of a simple profit and loss account.

William Wordsworth (1770-1850), a leading English Romantic poet, was born in 1770, as the second of five children of John Wordsworth, who was a legal representative of James Lowther, 1st Earl of Lonsdale. His mother, Anne, died of a malignant cold at the age of 30, when William was 7 years old. Five years after mother's death, his father, John, died of overwork at the age of 42. Not welcomed by relatives, William and his siblings were forced to leave their home and lost the foundation of the family. William went to St John's College, Cambridge University, but it is easy to imagine that he felt alienated by being discriminated against, based on status as a minority special scholarship student in a dormitory with many aristocrats and upper-class youths. While in college, he embarked on a three-month walking trip to the Alps of continental Europe. After graduating from Cambridge, he hoped to pursue a career in literature. He traveled to Wales and climbed Mount Snowdon. In 1791, he went to the continent again. This time, he wanted to learn French and become a private tutor who would take the children of the upper aristocracy on trips to France. Eventually, he met a French woman, Annette Vallon, who was four years older than him, who taught him French for free, and they became romantically involved. Vallon eventually gave birth to their daughter Caroline upon William's return to England. After that, the Anglo-French War made it impossible for him to go to France, and his dream of teaching on continental travel disappeared. Before long, Wordsworth sympathized with William Godwin's *Political Justice* and became an atheist, supporting the French Revolution. In 1795, he published a weekly magazine, *The Philanthropist*, dealing with political criticism and political thought. However, 6 months after the publication of the magazine, Wordsworth quit publishing the magazine, and at the same time, gave up on Godwin, disliked revolutionary terrorism, and distanced himself from left-wing communism. He sought the beauty of nature and the value of everyday life. He deepened his philosophical contemplation and devoted himself to the inner soul of man, the essence of nature, and religious thoughts. He longed for a life like a recluse who lives a simple life and thinks deeply about Almighty God. In 1798, he co-authored with Samuel Taylor Coleridge (1772-1834) in *Lyrical Ballads*. Wordsworth's 'Lines written a few miles above Tintern Abbey' adorned the end of the collection of poems. The origins of Wordsworth's idea were deeply rooted in the poor and oppressed lives of the lower class people in rural areas. Every subject of poetical works was the suffering and poverty of the people. Main characters were old men, unhappy women, and unfortunate boys. There was no social relief for the poor and weak. However, Wordsworth sought salvation and healing from nature, getting close to nature, looking at himself, and deepening his thoughts. He realized that nature never betrayed him.

William Wordsworth

According to Wordsworth's thought, if you experience walking in the great nature that has a majestic and sublime beauty, you would think that both rich and poor are the same, and there is not much difference between them as very petty human beings in the great outdoors. In the 1801 revised edition of *Lyrical Ballads*, Wordsworth declared that the language of the work would be the ordinary language used by the middle and lower classes of society. He would use the language used by rural people in the English countryside. Just as Sir Walter Scott (1771-1832) focused on the spirit of chivalry in medieval history, Wordsworth sought to revive the spirit of Christianity in nature and in the countryside. Both of them were trying to show a way of life to those who had lost their humanity in a chaotic big city.

A quiet and peaceful park in a metropolitan area is an oasis for people, a place for the rebirth of their souls.

13. Churches in London

The Church of England gained independence from the Roman Catholic Church in the 16ᵗʰ century. In 1534, the Act of Supremacy declared King Henry VIII Supreme Head of the Church of England. The main doctrine of the Protestant Reformation was justification by faith alone. However, the Church of England values a tolerant spirit, persists in the faith of Mary, and practically follows Catholic doctrine and tradition.

St Paul's Cathedral

St Paul's Cathedral, a representative church belonging to the Church

St Paul's Cathedral, the seat of the Bishop of London

of England, has long been a landmark of the City of London. In Roman times, the Temple of Diana was located at this site in London, and a wooden church was later built on the site of the temple (607). The church was destroyed by fire in the 11th century (1087),

West front

Sir Christopher Wren

but in 1137, it was converted into a Norman stone cathedral by William the Conqueror. It was rebuilt several times since then, and in the 13th century, a Gothic cathedral was constructed. The building was also destroyed in the Great Fire of London in 1666. The current building of St Paul's Cathedral, was rebuilt by Sir Christopher Wren (1632-1723) over a period of 35 years from 1675 to 1710. Charles II commissioned Wren to rebuild the Baroque domed cathedral, which had been destroyed in the Great Fire of London. This is what we can still see today. Wren studied mathematics and astronomy at Oxford University and was a renowned scholar who designed and built the Sheldonian Theatre in his alma mater, Oxford in 1669. He was involved in the rebuilding and restoration of 52 churches in the City after the Great Fire of London. Among them, he built St Paul's Cathedral in imitation of St. Peter's Basilica in Rome. At the time of completion, Wren had already reached the advanced age of 78. This circular dome played an important role in composing the landscape beauty of the City of London. Without a doubt, St Paul's Cathedral is Wren's masterpiece. The current King Charles III and the former Princess Diana (1961-97) were married here (They officially divorced in 1996).

Westminster Abbey

This church is a masterpiece of Gothic architecture in London. "Westminster" means the minster of the west. "Minster" means a venerable and special church in England. In other words, Westminster means the Minster west of London, as opposed to St Paul's Cathedral, the eastern minster of London. It is said to be the most French of the Gothic churches in England. The symmetrical towers and geometric designs are also continental. By the 13th century, almost its present appearance was completely built. There is a legend that a Saxon king built the first church on Thorney Island (around present-day Westminster) on the Thames in the 7th century, but it is uncertain. By the time Edward the Confessor became King of England in 1042, it is clear that Abbey already existed there. The Confessor built a

Western façade

palace and a new monastery there. William the Conqueror was coronated at Westminster Abbey in 1066. Since then, all kings since William I, except Edward V and Edward VIII, have been coronated at Westminster Abbey.

The wedding of the current Prince William (1982-) and Catherine, Princess of Wales (1982-), took place in Westminster Abbey in April 2011. After the wedding, just like William's parents, Prince Charles and Diana's 1981 wedding, the couple traveled in a horse-drawn carriage on the road from Westminster Abbey to Buckingham

Palace to the crowd of a million people, and finally had an audience with the crowd from the balcony of Buckingham Palace. In May 2023, the coronation of King Charles III (1948-) and Queen Camilla (1947-) was held at Westminster Abbey. They also traveled to Buckingham Palace in

North entrance of the abbey

a golden carriage (The Gold State Coach), appeared on the balcony, and received the blessings of the people who had gathered in front of the palace. It was lovely to see William, the Prince of Wales and Princess Catherine, as well as their children, Prince George (2013-), Princess Charlotte (2015-), and Prince Louis (2018-).

During the reign of Henry VIII, the abbey was abolished and became a royal church. Therefore, it is officially called "Collegiate Church of Saint Peter at Westminster". Most of the kings of England were buried here. Since the beginning of the 18th century, monuments have been built here to honor famous people from all walks of life. Or, some famous people, like Sir Isaac Newton (1642-1727), were actually buried. In one corner of the cathedral is Poet's Corner, which commemorates poets and writers. There are marble statues of Shakespeare, busts of Dr. Johnson, and monuments to John Milton (1608-1674), who was the great poet of the Renaissance, Wordsworth and other Romantic poets. Jane Austen, the Brontë sisters, Dickens, Hardy, Lewis Carroll, and D.H. Lawrence are also enshrined. Only a few were actually buried rather than memorials, such as Chaucer and Dr. Johnson. Chaucer, "the father of English poetry", was the first writer to be buried in Poets' Corner in 1400.

Chaucer, author of *The Canterbury Tales*

Geoffrey Chaucer (1340s-1400) was born in London and became one of the great poets of the Middle Ages in England. Perhaps his birthplace was Thames Street, in the Vintry ward of the City. At that time, the area was an area where wine shops were gathered and wealthy merchants lived. It was around Vintners Place, north of present-day Southwark Bridge. Chaucer's father, John Chaucer, was an important wine merchant with a royal appointment, and his family lived in a three-story stone house.

> Whan that Aprill, with his shoures soote
>
> The droghte of March hath perced to the roote,
>
> And bathed every veyne in swich licuor
>
> Of which vertu engendred is the flour,[26]

From *The Canterbury Tales*

Geoffrey Chaucer

When Chaucer was a child, the Black Death attacked London. But Chaucer escaped death by a miracle. He survived, and later on, a clever son of a merchant, Geoffrey, could work in the court as a page. Educated as a squire, he became a government official involved in accounting, law, and diplomatic mission. Chaucer was also a court poet, and he started his literary work as a translator. His first translation was French *Le Roman de la Rose* into English for the people of the court, especially the court ladies. He was good at Latin, Italian, and French. His artistic sensibility was nurtured by the French Literature and the Italian art. However, most of his works were written in English. His greatness is that he did not adopt the language of French or Latin, but that of the language used by the common people in England. He had a genuine literary sense and valued the more manly and expressive Anglo-Saxon language. He thought English was his mother tongue and it was a national language. Chaucer used the dialect of East Midlands, especially London-based English, which was also spoken in the area of Oxford and Cambridge. His masterpiece, *The Canterbury Tales*, was written in the 1390s, composed of more than 17,000 lines, by using about 30 percent of French words. *The Canterbury Tales* is a collection of episodes told by the people of different classes traveling together from Southwark in London to Canterbury. In *The Canterbury Tales*, the characters talked about lovely stories with each other on the way to their destination, Canterbury Cathedral. Those pilgrims had many kinds of occupations such as a wife of Bath, knight, miller, cook, man of law, friar, clerk (a student of Oxford), merchant, squire, franklin, physician, shipman, prioress, nun's priest, nun, parson, monk, and so on. Chaucer described medieval people's way of thinking and behaviors ironically or satirically. His interest was concentrated in humans. Chaucer's English is Middle English, and is an extremely important historical resource for those studying the history of the English language. It can be comparable to Shakespeare's English, a representative of Early Modern English.

Church of St Mary-Le-Bow and Cockney

The Church of St Mary-le-Bow is a Church of England parish church in the City of London. The current building was rebuilt in 1670 by Sir Christopher Wren after the Great Fire of London (1666). This church is one of the most famous churches in London because it is associated with the English language of Cockney. It is a church that anyone who studies English history or is interested in English linguistics knows.

> 'Davy, dear. If I ain't ben azackly as intimate with you. Lately, as I used to be. It ain't because I don't love you. Just as well and more, my pretty poppet. It's because I thought it better for you.[27]
>
> From *David Copperfield*

If you read Dickens' work, you will find Cockney English spoken in London at the time. Cockney is one of the typical English dialects that had spread in the East End, London. It was the language that was spoken by working-class people living in the East End since the early 19th century. The etymology of Cockney originally refers to a poorly shaped egg that looks like it was born by a rooster, or a cock. In the Middle Ages, it was a term that meant a soft and spoiled boy who grew up in the City of London. Later, at the end of the 15th century, it referred to those who were born within hearing of the bells of the church called St Mary-le-Bow in the City. In the 17th century, it referred to the common people who lived in London for generations. In the 18th and 19th centuries, after the Industrial Revolution, workers flocked to London, especially into the East End, so the word, Cockney, came to refer to these uneducated workers.

Their way of pronunciation was very unique and sometimes difficult to understand: *I don't know* would be "I donno." They pronounce *a* [ei] as [ai]: for example, *able* is pronounced as [aibi] and *day* is as [dai]. *Th* is pronounced as [f] or [v]: *theatre* is as "featre", *think* is as "fink", and *that* is as "vat", *with* is as "wiv". Also, they don't pronounce *h* sound in a word. For example, *half* is pronounced as [a:f], *happy* is as [æpi], *has* is as [az], *he* is [i:], *head* is [ed], *health* is [elƟ], *house* is [æus], and humble is as [ʌmbl]. If the indefinite article is added, they pronounce *a* as "an": for example, *a hand* is like [ənænd]. Cockney English does not pronounce [h], but on the contrary, some people are too concerned that they sometimes make an effort to add [h] sound when they don't need to pronounce it. For example, *ever* is [hevə]. Between vowels, there may be a non-existent [r] sound: for example, *America is* is pronounced like "America ris".

Cockney English also has many hidden expressions. They prefer expressions that could only be understood among them. For example, *Adam and Eve* means "believe". *Could you Adam and Eve it?* means "Could you believe it?". What's interesting is that *Eve* and (beli)*eve* rhyme each other. In general, there are many hidden nouns in Cockney, and they rhyme with endings. For example, *Bread and Honey* means Mo*ney*, *Donkey's Ears* means Y*ears*, *Lady Godiva* means Fi*ver* (5 pound note), *Pony* means 25 *pound*s, *Tea leaf* stands for Th*ief.*

As the Irish people can say, *my* in the sentence can be said, "me." This is also Cockney English. For example, *me heart* can be "my heart" and *meself* is "myself". Short forms of "am not," "are

View from Cheapside

133

not," "is not," "have not," and "has not" will all be *ain't*. As for *ain't*, which often appears in Irish English or Black English in America, it first appeared in London, in 1706. It was used in the sense of "am not" in the early 19ᵗʰ century, and it came to be used in the meaning of "aren't" and "isn't" in the Cockney dialect of London.

Today, it is said that many young Londoners think it's cool to speak Cockney, and people who are not working-class and don't live in the East End tend to speak Cockney.

Britain lost America due to the American Revolution War (1775-83) and lost the prisoner destinations it had been doing since 1717. Then, it was Australia that became the place to send criminals instead of America. In 1788,

about 750 prisoner men and women were first transported from England to Australia. Many immigrants, including "free" settlers, used Cockney dialect and Irish English. By 1900, the population of Australia was about 4 million. Australians often use their slang, for example, *Aussie* for *Australian*. Cockney is also widely used, but television announcers and newscasters don't speak Cockney.

Black English is now called African-American English in the

Bicycles lined up in front of the church

USA. The first African slaves arrived

in Virginia in 1619. Then in the 17th century, many black slaves were shipped from West Africa to America. And then, after the American Civil War (1861-65), over 4 million African slaves eventually became free. When I read American literature, I sometimes confirm they said like this, "An I ain't no plan," or "I ain't got no chance," instead of "And I haven't no plan," or "I don't have any chance." I think the reason why they used *ain't* instead of *am not, isn't, aren't, haven't*, and *hasn't* is because of the influence of Cockney, which once came to the United States from London. Not pronouncing the *t* sound in American English is also a feature of Cockney English. I wonder if the fact is also the influence of Cockney.

Today, Christians in the UK are said to be about 60% of the population. However, only about one in ten of them go to church every week, and at most one in five people go to church about once a month. Less than 10% of the population follow other religions, including Muslims, Hindus, and Buddhists, and about 25% have no religion. It is also said that young people rarely go to church. Many churches are in danger of closing the church, selling of historical buildings, or demolition due to financial difficulties to keep the building. Nonetheless, the coronations of kings and queens, royal weddings, Christmas events, relief efforts for homeless people, and charity events for the poor suggest that Christianity is firmly rooted in British culture and British life. And Christianity is still involved in people's everyday life, and connected to citizens than Japanese Buddhism and Shintoism. I think British Christian culture still deeply influences their way of life.

14. Transportation in London

At Waterloo we were fortunate in catching a train for Leatherhead, where we hired a trap at the station inn, and drove for four or five miles through the lovely Surrey lanes. It was a perfect day, with a bright sun and a few fleecy clouds in the heavens. The trees and wayside hedges were just throwing out their first green shoots, and the air was full of the pleasant smell of the moist earth.[28]   'The Speckled Band'

The mainstream of transportation before and after the Industrial Revolution was sailing ships that used wind power, and later steamboats that used steam engines appeared. When it comes to land transportation, horse-drawn carriages (such as railroad carriages) were popular. The horse-drawn carriage called the omnibus, first appeared in 1829. The railroad horse-drawn carriage was eventually replaced by the steam locomotive. Canals, which were waterways, crisscrossed the land, and canal boats played the role of water transportation. There were also canal boats drawn by horses. The canal declined with the advent of the railway in

The Tube running on the ground   Inside the Tube

the 19th century. Today, some of them remain as recreational cruising. The energy that moved the vehicle became coal from horsepower and wind power in the 19th century. Then, in the 20th century, the age of oil came, and the automobile appeared. Those bright red double-decker buses and black boxed taxis are probably the best of London's specialties. These two vehicles undoubtedly give the City of London its vitality, beauty and charm. Just as horse-drawn carriages and one-horse carriages used to liven up the streets of London in the 19th century, red buses and black taxis replaced them in the 20th century.

Double-Decker Bus

The first double-decker (bus) appeared in London in 1904. Initially, there was no roof, and the roof of the bus didn't appear until 1925. The word *bus* was originally spelled *omnibus* in the sense of a shared carriage or shared car, but it was abbreviated as *bus*. The etymology comes from the Latin word meaning "for everyone". This is not possible with current buses, but the old red buses had steps at the rear and I could jump off and hop on (the rear open deck has been abolished since 2007). The new double-decker of the current one-man system appeared in the late 1960s, but the old model remained until the late 1990s. Speaking of double decker, it is an image of a London route bus, but outside London, it is operated not only in major cities in the UK, but also former colonies, such

Double-deckers running in front of Big Ben

as Hong Kong, Singapore, India, Canada, etc. It is also operated as an express bus and sightseeing bus in Japan, South Korea, China, Taiwan, and so on.

London Taxi, Black Cab

The origin of the word "cab" comes from the cabriolet, which was a new type of coach from France in the 19th century. The horse-drawn carriage (unit) became the first automobile in 1904. Then the history of London taxis started. The Austin brand, also known as the Black Cab, has recently undergone a major facelift. From the conventional box shape, it has a streamlined and soft appearance. The biggest change is that all taxicabs (about 20,000) in London will be electrified, in anticipation of the UK banning the sale of engine-powered cars by 2035. In addition, the color of the car body is gradually incorporating various colors from all black. A "wrapping advertisement" vehicle also appeared. Drivers are also dressed more casually than before. The company changed its name from The London Taxi Company to London Electric Vehicle Company, or LEVC for short. The next-generation new taxi is said to be the LEVC TX (electric vehicle). By the way, in order to become a taxi driver in London, you have to pass a difficult exam. In addition to the two-class car license, there is an exam called The Knowledge of London, which you cannot pass without various knowledge of the City

of London. It is said to be the most difficult taxi driver test in the world. As for taxi tips, unlike in the United States, it doesn't mean that you always have to give a tip to the driver. However, a fraction of the fare may be rounded up and you may give extra money to the driver. Of course, if the service is very good, such as being very responsive or helping to load and unload heavy luggage, you can tip as a thank you. I remember that when I was young, I once took a taxi in London and tried to tip about 10 percent of the fare. The driver kindly said, "You're young, you're still a student, you can tip only when you can earn more," and he didn't accept the tip.

Railway

England is the birthplace of railways. The history of British railways began in 1802 when Richard Trevithick (1771-1833), a British engineer born in Cornwall, invented the world's first steam locomotive. In fact, the world's first railway opened for the Stockton and Darlington Railway in north east England in 1825, and a passenger railway began in 1830, making it the oldest line in the world. After World War I, the 120 railway companies were consolidated into four companies, and after World War II, they were nationalized. It was privatized in 1997. Originally known as British Railways, after 1969 known as British Rail (BR), now it is called National Rail. The high-speed train is called Inter City, which is equivalent to a bullet train in Japan. But there is no express charges like Japan's JR. There is a sleeper train on the line between London and Scotland, which is called the sleeper service.

Windsor & Eton Riverside Station

Underground

The London Underground is called the Underground, or the Tube, by locals. The origin of the London Underground is the Metropolitan Railway, which opened in 1863 (closed in 1933). It terminated at Paddington, Euston, and King's Cross to the City. Towed by a steam locomotive, the inside of the tunnel was turned black with soot. Perhaps they ran underground instead of above ground because people feared that the City of London would be full of soot. The modern Underground was constructed in the 1890s. In 1902, it was operated by the Underground Electric Railways Company of London. In 1933, the London Passenger Transport Board (LPTB) was created. Since 2003, the

London Underground has been part of Transport for London (TfL).

TfL also outsources operations to double-decker operating companies. Nowadays, an IC card called the Oyster Card can be used at a discount on the Underground and bus services, but not on the Heathrow Express and National Rail. Also, as an overall impression, the station staff are very well-mannered, and they seem to be polite and work with some pride. It also seems that their job is not only to make the trains run on time, but to prioritize getting passengers to their destinations safely. In Japan, train operating companies tend to place too much emphasis on keeping trains on time. This is something I thought about many times when I travelled in England by British Rail.

Bicycle

In the UK, commuting allowances are basically not paid. And these days, perhaps in consideration of health consciousness, alleviation of traffic congestion, and measures to address global environmental issues, bicycle commuting seems to be popular in London. Currently, bicycle users outnumber car users as a means of transportation during peak traffic times in London. The British government is also actively subsidizing the purchase of bicycles. There is a government-approved bicycle rental service that can be used easily. Bicycles are also popular among tourists. You'll often see bicycles named after their sponsor (a financial institution) named Santander. The reason why bicycles are so popular in London is probably due to the climate. Unlike Japan in summer, the temperature is low and the air is dry, so even if you ride a bicycle,

you won't sweat so much. Would you ride a bicycle every day on your commute in a hot and humid summer in Japan?

Airplane

Heathrow Airport

Finally, I would like to mention Heathrow, the UK's largest airport on the western edge of London. Speaking of airplanes, the American Wright Brothers succeeded in the world's first manned flight with a propeller attached to the engine in 1903, and also an American Charles Lindbergh (1902-74) made a successful transatlantic flight with a propeller aircraft. Regarding airplane development, the image of the United States is strong, and in Europe, the image of Germany and France is strong because Germany developed the jet engine (1939), and a Frenchman named Louis Bériot (1872-1936) created the Blériot XI, the world's first airplane to fly across the English Channel in 1909.

Antoine de Saint-Exupéry (1900-44) and his work, *Le Petit Prince* (1943) also have a clearer image of the relationship between France and airplanes. However, the world's first jetliner, de Havilland Comet, was put into service by the United Kingdom (1952). And again, American jumbo jet, or Boeing 747 appeared (1969). In 1976, the Concorde, a supersonic airliner jointly developed by the United Kingdom and France, began flying (commercial flights ended in 2003). Unmanned aerial vehicles (or drones) have appeared in recent years. Is the United States still playing a central role in this field as well?

London Heathrow Airport dates back to 1929. At that time, the first airfield was built there. During World War II, it was requisitioned by the Royal Air Force and returned to the Ministry of Civil Aviation after the war. In 1959, it became an international airport. In 1977, the London Underground Piccadilly line opened.

Following the privatization policy of the Thatcher government, the British Airports Authority (BAA) was privatized in 1987. The Heathrow Express between the airport and Paddington station in London opened in 1998, and the slightly slower but cheaper Heathrow Connect opened in 2005. Since Virgin Atlantic Airways closed and withdrew its branch of Japan in 2015, British Airways became the only British airline to fly to Japan. Privatized in 1987, British Airways is the UK's largest airline with Heathrow as its main hub. It was also British Airways that put into service the world's first jet airliner Comet and put into service the world's first supersonic passenger aircraft Concorde.

When I first visited England 30 years ago, it was about to land, and as the aircraft made a big turn, I looked out the window and saw cute two-story brick houses that looked like something out of a fairy tale, with chimneys and green lawns, lined up in a street without power poles. I still vividly remember thinking what a fashionable country I had come to, looking out the window of the British Airways plane.

British Airways check-in counter at Heathrow Airport

15. The Food of the Individualist British People

It is commonly said, even by the English themselves, that English cooking is the worst in the world. It is supposed to be not merely incompetent, but also imitative, and I even read quite recently, in a book by a French writer, the remark: 'The best English cooking is, of course, simply French cooking.'[29]

In Defence of English Cooking by George Orwell

The monotony of British cuisine is basically due to the fact that Britain is a northern country and the land is not fertile, so agricultural products are scarce. The British are predominantly Anglo-Saxon, and their lives are basically frugal. When it comes to food, they value quantity over quality, and the British diet is based on "gluttony and gulp (eating a lot and drinking a lot)". As a result, traditionally, many of the dishes are so simple that one suspects that the British are not very interested in food. Basically, there was a belief that if you can eat until your stomach is full, that's great. Compared to France, Italy and Spain, the cuisine in Britain is clearly frugal. England was historically somewhat rich compared to Scotland, but very little as good as the continental southern European countries. However, you can enjoy the original taste of the ingredients as much as you can. Emphasis is placed on food ingredients, and the seasoning is relatively light. Of course, historically, aristocrats would eat French food in their castles. They didn't drink whiskey, beer, gin, etc., but they enjoyed drinking fine wine.

English breakfast

Speaking of traditional British breakfasts, it is called "English breakfast" (in Scotland they say "Scottish breakfast"). It's a full course that fills your stomach, consisting of oatmeal (porridge), bacon and eggs, two slices of toast, honey, marmalade, blueberry jam, and milk tea (these are the basic menu). There are also fish dishes such as dover sole, smoked herring (kipper), and smoked salmon. Options include hashed potatoes, mushrooms, small grilled tomatoes, beans, scrambled eggs, sausages, orange juice and coffee. In the past, eating sandwiches at pubs for lunch was still a luxurious meal, and some college students ate only a chocolate and an apple for lunch. I had an acquaintance who enjoyed drinking milk tea with biscuits at high tea for dinner and went to bed. It is said that many British people went to bed after eating light meals for dinner. Their diet is supported by hearty breakfasts, and during my travels around the UK, I relied on them as my main source of nutrition, that is to say, essentially one meal a day. In Japan, sometimes I don't want to eat such a greasy breakfast in the morning, but it is probably because I have a lot of dinner the day before, and my stomach is upset. When I wake up in the morning without dinner, I can realize how greasy, high-calorie breakfast I can eat. Of course, British eating habits these days have shifted to continental breakfasts or American styles. Many people get by with toast, cereal, and coffee. I've never heard of an office worker eating an English breakfast every weekday.

Fish and chips

Fish and chips, or battered fish with chips, are a signature dish of England. Fish and chips are often eaten as an ordinary household dish and in restaurants. But if you eat them in a London restaurant, it's ridiculously expensive. In the past,

Fish and chips served at home in London

they were often sold at takeout shops. White fish such as cod is battered with flour, eggs and water, fried, and served with potato fries. Fish and chips were a popular meal throughout Britain after the Industrial Revolution. In the past, stalls were everywhere in London, wrapped in newspaper and eaten casually, but the use of newspaper is now banned due to hygiene issues. In recent years, overfishing has made it difficult for people to obtain cod and costs also go up. More and more foreign fast-food chains are increasing sales, and fish and chips are served on plates at London restaurants for a hefty price. They are often eaten with salt and vinegar by Londoners.

Sunday roast

Sunday roast is a home-cooked meat dish eaten for Sunday lunch. This includes roast beef, potatoes, Yorkshire pudding, and vegetables. Originally, landowners thanked the serfs for one week of labor, and they gave their serfs

Pub, "Edward VII" in London

Sunday roast

roast beef on Sundays. Especially, after the Industrial Revolution, the Sunday roast that became available in Yorkshire is very famous. It is now eaten all over the UK. Chicken, duck, lamb, and pork are sometimes used instead of beef. You can eat Sunday roast casually not at restaurants but at pubs that serve food.

Pie cooking

In Japan, we associate pie with sweet desserts such as apple pie, cheese pie, strawberry pie, pumpkin pie, pear pie, and other pies wrapped in sweetly boiled fruit. But British pie is originally eaten for lunch or dinner. It is called British pie, shepherd's pie, or cottage pie, which is a meat pie made from minced beef (or mutton), onions and tomatoes, wrapped in mashed potatoes and baked in the oven. There is also a meat pie called pasty (or Cornish pasty), which is wrapped in a dumpling-like shape and baked that originated in the Cornwall region. However, like Christmas pudding, mince pie, which was originally eaten with minced meat, is now a sweet food of apples and fruit wrapped in puff pastry and baked, which is eaten as a dessert. A prime example would be apple pie. The dish pictured on this page is a traditional mince beef (pie) with mashed potatoes, served at "Mother Mash" in London.

"Mother Mash" in London

Mince beef pie

Sandwich

Sandwiches are a food derived from a real British aristocrat, John Montagu, 4th Earl of Sandwich (1718-1792). Of course, the custom of eating meat between bread would have already existed not only in other parts of the world, but also in Britain. However, it was the Earl of Sandwich who popularized this word to the world as the name of such food. He took over the title of Earl of Sandwich in 1728 at the age of only 10. The Earl became an able politician and also served as Postmaster General of the United Kingdom, First Lord of the Admiralty, and Secretary of State for the Northern Department. On the other hand, he was a gambler, and he hated taking a break from gambling to eat, so he ordered his butler to bring meat between bread so that he could eat while playing cards. Gradually, this became popular with his friends, and eventually such bread (putting a filling between two slices of bread) was called "sandwiches". The reason why this word has become established as a word for sandwiches is not that the name of the inventor of the food happened to be Earl of Sandwich, but that it is a food invented by the gambling-loving Earl to spare no time to eat, and this

Earl of Sandwich

episode seems humorous as the etymology of sandwich. Furthermore, the word "Earl" even conveys a sense of luxury in the food. But perhaps the biggest reason why the name of the Earl of Sandwich became the name of the food was that John Montagu himself had a wonderful personality that made him attractive as a person. I don't care if the etymology of negative words is negative (e.g., brute, melancholy, trauma). But it's important to make a good impression when people say something delicious and fun, when they eat at a picnic or lunch, or when they refer to exciting food. I think sandwich is a very attractive name.

Afternoon tea

Tea that came to Japan from China came to be called "cha". This is probably derived from "cha-ina". In 1613, merchants of the British East India Company set up a trading house in Hirado, Kyushu, Japan, and began trading with Japan. At that time, Japanese green tea, "cha", was brought back to England for the first time. "Cha" eventually came to be called "tae" and then "tea". In fact, the history of English tea can be said to begin in 1662. In that year, the Portuguese Infanta Catherine de Braganza (1638-1705), came to the British royal family from Portugal to become queen of Charles II, bringing tea, a luxury item at the time, as part of her dowry. She enjoyed drinking tea every day. Then tea became popular at the court. Initially, green tea with sugar was enjoyed. After that, more fermented black tea with a bitter taste began to be imported, and the custom of

drinking black tea with sugar and milk took root. The custom of drinking black tea spread among the common people in the late 18th century. It was around this time that Wedgwood and Minton's bone china tea sets began

Cake stand

Duchess of Bedford

149

Wedgwood Wild Strawberry Set

to be produced.

The history of afternoon tea dates back to the 1840s. Anna Maria Russell, 7th Duchess of Bedford (1783-1857), made it a habit to have the servant prepare sandwiches and cakes to be accompanied by tea to satisfy a little hunger between lunch and dinner (around 4 o'clock in the afternoon). Eventually, she began inviting friends to enjoy them together. It became popular and became a fashionable social event in high society. The invited ladies wore long dresses, gloves and hats. In the second half of the 19th century, it spread not only to the upper class but also to the middle class. Today, afternoon tea usually starts at 3 a.m. Enjoy an afternoon tea in the tea lounge of one of London's top hotels, and you'll be able to fully enjoy the traditions of the good old days of the Victorian era. Or you can enjoy it more casually at a regular restaurant or café. There are four types of black tea available: traditional tea (a traditional afternoon tea with a rich aroma and full-bodied, which is a blend of Indian tea and Ceylon tea), Indian tea (Darjeeling tea and Assam tea), Ceylon tea, and Chinese black tea (Earl Grey tea,

Casual restaurant in London

Keemun tea, Lapsang Suochong tea). The tea that the British drink is basically milk tea. Then comes the three-tiered cake stand. From the bottom level, there are thin bread sandwiches such as rye (cucumber, eggs, smoked salmon, roast beef, cheese, etc. are sandwiched), scones (with a small jar of jam, clotted cream, and butter), and small cakes (fruit cake or sponge cake). In the three plates, the food is arranged so that the more it moves to the upper tier, the sweeter the taste of the food becomes. Reservations are required at

A cafe in Yokohama, Japan

hotels, and basically, reservations can be made from two or more people. But you can also enjoy afternoon tea alone at restaurants and cafés in London.

My teacher, Prof. Deguchi, once published many books on British tea, and was a contributor who established the correct knowledge of British tea in Japan. He was the first to spread British tea culture to Japan. Before him, lemon tea had been the mainstream tea in Japan. Maybe, the tea culture of Japan was probably tea via Russia. At the time, we didn't know that the British didn't drink hot lemon tea, they drank milk tea. For us graduate students of Waseda University, whether in the university professor's laboratory or at his home, Prof. Deguchi always treated us to afternoon tea with biscuits, cakes, or sandwiches. I had been indebted to him for over 30 years. In other words, that is, I had been allowed to drink British tea brewed by him for almost 30 years. I think my body is partly made of British tea brewed by Professor Deguchi.

British pub

"Pub" stands for "public house", and in the middle of the 19th century, this word appeared. The pub was a tavern (bar) and became a social gathering place for commoners, which mainly served beer. Now, you can drink a variety of drinks in the pub, and the variety of food has also been served as a menu. A sign with a square picture is always displayed above the entrance of the pub. There are many unique pub names: for example, Bank Tavern, The Bleeding Wolf, The Black Friars (monk), The Headless Woman, Hole in the Wall, King's Head, The Prince of Wales, Queen's Head, Mad Dog, Nobody Inn, The Pub with No Names, The Roaring Donkey, Union Pub, and so on. Originally, a cheap inn for tourists, did not have enough business and income, so they began to serve alcohol and meals for the locals, and eventually it became a social gathering place for people living in local towns and villages. Today's pub style was established in the early 20th century. There are still pubs in the countryside where you can stay. Fish and chips and roast beef are also standard dishes and can be eaten there. Basically, it is a style called cash on delivery, in which customers order drinks and food at the counter, pay for them, and receive the drink. As soon as the food is ready, the waiter will bring it to the table. On weekends, the pub is very crowded, and

many customers eat, drink, and chat loudly while standing. These days, there are many pubs that have several large screen TVs for customers to watch sports' games like soccer, rugby, and tennis.

Modern British

The UK basically has a national character that is thoroughly individualistic, and it is a culture that values the individual more than the group. Others are not involved in other people's personal matters or privacy. They don't have the basic principle of behavior like Japanese people, that is, "everyone else does it, so do I." They don't care much about what other people are eating. The reason why the food is basically lightly seasoned is probably to give your own flavor to the food on the plate. British food is bad if you don't season it your way yet. You are the one who finishes the dish. On the other hand, in addition to traditional British cuisine, modern British cuisine has recently been increasingly popular, with fashionable and delicious meals influenced by French cuisine and Mediterranean cuisine such as Italy and Spain. In addition to seafood such as squid and octopus, dishes using raw fish also appeared. Soy sauce and miso flavors also appeared. It is also important to satisfy the stomachs of overseas gourmet tourists who come to the UK. It can be said that the British national character, which is based on traditional culture but does not forget the spirit of constant improvement, and which does not like revolution and likes reform, also influences their food culture. Don't you think so?

"Rules", London's oldest restaurant

Conclusion

Once, when I traveled frequently to England and traveled around each region extensively and came back to London again, I would sometimes think of the destruction of the British Empire, which was once said to be the land where the sun never sets, on the way to the hotel where I was going to stay that day, taking in the views of London before my eyes. Marble buildings lining the streets, a lot of bronze statues, sumptuous and graceful appearances reminiscent of the prosperity of Athens and the Roman Empire, clusters of Neo-Gothic architecture built in the Victorian era, a large young man wearing a dirty green uniform and cleaning expressionlessly under the building, a white-collar man and woman leaving the office after working hours, a female vagrant burst out of nowhere as the office entrance closed and the shutters came down, homeless people wandering on the streets... Looking at such a cold scene, I couldn't help but feel that civilization always has an end. Britain in front of me was indeed sick. I thought it was definitely dying. However, because the accumulation of the past was great and enormous, they did not know that their country would be easily destroyed. Britain was being given its life, but it was definitely coming to an end. I felt that there was no sign of recovery. Some emphasized their mental richness rather than material affluence. Certainly, compared to many Japanese who were not independent enough like children, I thought they were much more self-confident, open-minded, and humorous adults. However, even in such a situation, England was definitely in decline. I keenly realized that the only thing they could do was to quietly watch over the existence

of the culture and civilization
built by their ancestors for as long
as possible with a generous heart. I
thought of the inevitability of
change, the inevitability of being
born in this world, flourishing,
declining, and finally leaving the
stage.

Alnwick Castle in Northumberland, England

"We don't have a job anymore", the middle-aged woman told me in Hyde
Park. Her words never left my mind for a long time. I used to give cash to the
elderly alcoholic men who came up to me while waiting at the bus stop. Under
a cloudy evening sky, there were Londoners strolling through the City, which
was full of car exhaust and dust. Everyone was truly unique and walked in
various ways. There was a young woman wearing revealing clothes, so I didn't
think that she was coming home from the office. There was a young man with
many piercings in his ears, and a girl who walked with a ring hanging from her
nose. The advancement of people of color was also conspicuous.

London is a melting pot of humanity; the collapse of the family, rising
sexual crime rates, widespread plague, constant laughter in the pub, never-
ending cheerful conversations, white vagrants wandering under the majestic
bronze statues towering in the sky, and a large number of tourists from all over
the world enjoying sightseeing. I felt like I had caught a glimpse of the profile
of an Englishman who had blown away his dying homeland with laughter and
slowly advanced to the land of eternal comfort. I felt as if I had learned the
aesthetics of perdition when I came to England. Everything in this world is
doomed to perish. An era ends, and a new era begins. The Roman Empire had

fallen and vanished, but the salvation lies in the fact that Italians enjoy life to the fullest. They live cheerfully, passionately, and happily.

With the popularity of Romanticism in the 19th century, the British regained a fascination with medieval spirit (Christianity) and medieval Gothic architecture. Especially during this period, the reconstruction and restoration of the church and castle, flourished. At that time, people were especially attached to medieval castle ruins and preferred to use the expression "picturesque beauty". After many battles and conflicts, the castle building withstood the winds and snows of the times, and eventually, the lord who lived there was gone, the floor collapsed, the stone walls collapsed, and the ruins of the castle were once again decorated with fresh green ivy leaves in early spring. The British like such contrasting scenery of old and new, war and peace, honor and betrayal, glory and destruction, the human world and the natural world, and what man made and what God created, etc. At that time, the Gothic Revival movement, which aimed at the restoration and reconstruction of the medieval world, flourished everywhere in Britain. Good examples are the British Houses of Parliament, Tower Bridge, Arundel Cathedral in West Sussex, Cardiff Castle and Caerphilly Castle in Wales, and Abbotsford Walter Scott's House in Scotland.

At first glance, this attitude of recreating the lost past seems to be going against the times, but it is not. It can be said that it is an act of re-examining and reviving values that have already become an idea of the past, and helping to break the deadlock. Of course, it was not only a physical restoration, but also a restoration of lost morality, humanity, Christian spirit, and love of God. While the British people chase the cutting edge of science and technology, they are a people who are very obsessed with the past. That is their toughness, their sense of balance, and the secret to their lives without perishing easily. There may be opportunities for victory, success, and prosperity in the future.

As represented by Winston Churchill and Dr. Johnson, the British are tough. However, there are many people who are not only indomitable and strong, or not only brilliant, but also charming and somehow unhateful in their actions, manners, and statements. Overall, even the most outrageous scholars and politicians have one thing in common: a sense of humor. They have elegance in their rough character, and a sense of humor in their arrogant attitudes. They are often multifaceted and multi-talented people. The collection started by a doctor living in London named Hans Sloane as a hobby led to the world's biggest British museum, and Marshal Wellington, the hero who defeated Napoleon, became Prime Minister. Sir Winston Churchill, a great politician, won the Nobel Prize in Literature. Perhaps their distant ancestors were Iberians, Celts, Vikings, Anglo-Saxons, Normans, and various ethnic groups. In the end, the wild and powerful culture of the Germanic Anglo-Saxons and the elegant French culture were fused to settle down. They became a people with a remarkable sense of balance. In a male-dominated society, it has become a national character where female writers, such as Austen, the Brontë sisters, Agatha Christie, and J.K. Rowling, can play an active role.

I like the rose, which is the national flower of England. Roses are not only beautiful, but also have sharp thorns on the stems. Even if you reach out and try to rip it off just because it's beautiful, they won't let you do that. Rose flowers point their weapons at you when attacked. It is only when it combines beauty and strength that I can feel true beauty. The cherry blossoms that Japanese people like are easily separated from the branches and scattered just by the wind. Compared to the weak and pale beauty of cherry blossoms, the beauty of roses becomes even more obvious. The late Princess Diana was compared to an England's rose, but I think Queen Elizabeth II, who passed away last year, was also such a beautiful and strong English rose.

Recently, the British have become more health-conscious and are shifting their diet from meat to vegetarian. The terms veganism or vegan also originated in England in the 1940s. There are also many animal lovers. Dogs and cats kept at home are expressed using "he" and "she". In the Victorian era, there were many people who valued hard work as good, and were just like the "corporate warriors" of the Japan, during the bubble economy (1986-91). But after World War II, Britain became a welfare state, people became more home-based, the motivation to work declined, and people valued their individual lives more than before. One of the lifestyles of the British these days is to be quiet, modest, not luxurious, to enjoy everyday life and to live a long and healthy life. They value coexistence, co-prosperity, alleviation of conflicts with others, modest self-assertion, loving small animals, not fighting, liking reading, and living as quietly as possible. It smells somewhat religious, but it is a way of thinking ahead of the times. The last Saxon king, Edward the Confessor, was shy, did not like conflict, and only lived by reading the Bible. He was an incompetent king for his time, but his way of thinking resonates with people today, in some sense. In fact, it can be said that it was ahead of the time.

Diversity, understanding of minorities, etc. are often heard as keywords in social life these days, but I feel that many of the British people I have met so far are multifaceted on an individual level, and that there are many people who have diverse values coexisting within themselves, and I also want to be that kind of person.

NOTES

(1) Robert Hardman, *Queen of Our Times: The Life of Elizabeth II 1926-2022* (Pan Macmillan, 2022), p.639.

(2) Winston Spencer Churchill, *Memoirs of The Second World War* (Houghton Mifflin, 1987), pp.1015-1016.

(3) 夏目漱石『倫敦塔・幻影の盾』（新潮文庫 2021），8頁.

(4) Charles Dickens, *David Copperfield* (Penguin Classics, 2004), p.178.

(5) J. E. Morpurgo, *Keats* (Penguin Poetry Library, 1953), p.67.

(6) *Ibid.*, p.177.

(7) Charles Dickens, *A Christmas Carol* (Puffin Classics, 1994), p.1.

(8) Helen Vendler, *The Art of Shakespeare's Sonnets* (The Belknap Press of Harvard University Press, 1997), p.119.

(9) N. F. Blake, *The Language of Shakespeare* (MacMillan, 1983), p.42., p.118.

(10) *Ibid.*, p.16., p.48.

(11) *Ibid.*, p.27.

(12) Frank Kermode, *Shakespeare's Language* (Penguin Books, 2000), p.52.

(13) *Ibid.*, p.96.

(14) Friedrich Nietzsche, *Also sprach Zarathustra* (Insel Klassik, 2011), p.315.

(15) Jean-Paul Sartre, *L'existentialisme est un humanisme* (Éditions Gallimard, 1996), p.26.

(16) G. L. Brook, *The Language of Shakespeare* (Andre Deutsch, 1976), p.68, p.76.

(17) Samuel Johnson, *The History of Rasselas, Prince of Abissinia* (Penguin Classics, 1976), pp.149-150.

(18) P. Austin Nuttall, *Johnson's Dictionary of the English Language, for the Use of Schools and General Students* (G. Routledge & Co., 1855), p.31.

(19) Samuel Johnson, *The History of Rasselas, Prince of Abissinia* (Penguin Classics, 1976), p. 65.

(20) Arthur Conan Doyle, *Sherlock Holmes Selected Stories* (Oxford University Press, 1980), p.207.

(21) J.K. Rowling, *Harry Potter and the Philosopher's Stone* (Bloomsbury, 2014), pp.95-96.

(22) *Ibid.*, p.129.

(23) Text of J.K. Rowling's speech from The Harvard Gazette, https://news. harvard. edu 2008/06.

(24) James Matthew Barrie, *Peter Pan in Kensington Gardens* (Independently published, 2022), p.1.

(25) Harold Bloom and Lionel Trilling, *Romantic Poetry and Prose* (Oxford University

Press, 1973), 128.

(26) Larry D. Benson, *The Riverside Chaucer* (Third Edition, Oxford University Press, 1988), p.23.

(27) Charles Dickens, *David Copperfield* (Penguin Classics, 2004), p.71.

(28) Arthur Conan Doyle, *Sherlock Holmes Selected Stories* (Oxford University Press, 1980), p.50.

(29) George Orwell, *In Defence of English Cooking* (Penguin Books, 1984), p.54.

Residential area on the outskirts of London

BIBLIOGRAPHY

Anderson, James, and G. Ross Roy. *Sir Walter Scott and History*, The Edina Press Lid., 1981.

Bentio, Fernando and Pedro Bentio. *The Handy London Map & Guide*. Bensons Mapguides Ltd, 2020.

Blake, N. F. *The Language of Shakespeare*, MacMillan Press Ltd., 1989.

Bloom, Harold and Lionel Trilling, *Romantic Poetry and Prose*, Oxford University Press, 1973.

Bowen, Zack. *Critical Essays on Sir Walter Scott: The Waverley Novels*, G. K. Hall & Co., 1996.

Bragg, Melvyn. *The Adventure of English: The Biography of a Language*, Hodder & Stoughton, 2003.

Brantlinger, Patrick, and William B. Thesing. *A Companion to The Victorian Novel*, Blackwell Publishing Lid, 2007.

British Museum. *Classic Reprint Series: The British Museum*, FB&c Ltd., 2015.

Brook, G. L. *The Language of Dickens*, Andre Deutsch, 1970.

——— *The Language of Shakespeare*, Andre Deutsch, 1976.

Brown, R. Allen. *Castles from the Air*, Cambridge University Press, 1989.

Carter, Ronald and John McRae. *Guide to English Literature: Britain and Ireland*, The Penguin, 1996.

Churchill, Winston Spencer. *Memoirs of The Second World War*, Houghton Mifflin, 1987.

Coghill, Nevill. *Geoffery Chaucer The Canterbury Tales*, Penguin Books, 1977.

Cohen, Susan. *London's Afternoon Teas: A Guide to the Most Exquisite Tea Venues in London*, IMM Lifestyle Books, 2018.

Craig, Edward. *Philosophy: A Very Short Introduction*, Oxford University Press, 2020.

Crump, Vincent and Leonie Glass. *Family Guide London*, Penguin Random House, 2018.

Davison, Brian. *The Observers Series-Castles*, Frederick Warne, 1988.

Deighton, H. S. *The Oxford Introduction to British History: A Portrait of Britain*, Oxford University Press, 1987.

Eagle, Dorothy and Hilary Carnell. *The Oxford Literary Guide to the British Isles*, Oxford University Press, 1977.

English Heritage. *The Blue Plaque Guide*, Journeyman Press, 1991.

Fallon, Steve, Damian Harper, and others. *Pocket London: Top Experiences • Local Life*, Lonely Planet Global Limited, 2022.

Forde-Johnston, James. *A Guide to the Castles of England and Wales,* Constable, 1989.

Gascoigne, Christina and Bamber. *Castles of Britain*, Thames and Hudson, 1992.

Hardman, Robert. *Queen of Our Times: The Life of Elizabeth II 1926-2022*, Pan Macmillan, 2022.

Harris, Nathaniel. *Castles of England Scotland and Wales A Guide and Gazetteer*, George Philip, 1991.

Humphries, P.H. *Castles of Edward the First in Wales*, HMSO, 1983.

Ingham, Patricia. *Dickens, women & language*, Harvester Wheatsheaf, 1992.

Jeffares, A. Norman. *Scott's Mind and Art*, Oliver & Boyd, 1969.

Johnson, Edgar. *Sir Walter Scott, The Great Unknown, Vol.1, Vol.2*, Hamish Hamilton, 1970.

Johnson, Keith. *Shakespeare's English*, Routledge, 2014.

Johnson, Paul. *Castles of England, Scotland and Wales*, Weidenfeld and Nicolson, 1992.

Kaye, Sharon. *Philosophy: A complete introduction*, Hodder & Stoughton, 2013.

Kermode, Frank. *Shakespeare's Language*, Penguin Books, 2000.

Kenny, Anthony. *A New History of Western Philosophy*, Oxford University Press, 2010.

Kerrigan, John. *The Sonnets and A Lover's Complaint by William Shakespeare*, Penguin Books, 1995.

King, D. J. Cathcart. *The Castle in England and Wales*, Croom Helm, 1988.

Kinross, John. *Discovering Castles in England and Wales*, Shire Publications, 1984.

Lamb, Charles. *Elia, 1823*, Woodstock Books, 1991.

Lindsay, Donald and E. S. Washington. *A Portrait of Britain 1688-1851*, Oxford University Press, 1984.

Lockhart, John Gibson. *The Life of Sir Walter Scott*, Hutchinson & Co., 1848.

McCrum, Robert, William Cran, and Robert MacNeil. *The Story of English: Third Revised Edition*, Faber & Faber, 2002.

Middleditch, Michael. *The Penguin London Mapguide*, Penguin Books, 1993.

Miller, Luree. *Literary Villages of London*, Starrhill Press, 1989.

Montague-Smith, Patrick W. *The Royal Line of Succession: The British Monarchy from Cerdic AD 534 to Queen Elizabeth II*, Pitkin Pictorials, 1995.

Monod, Sylvère. *Dickens the Novelist*, University of Oklahoma Press, 1968.

Morpurgo, J. E. *Keats*, Penguin Books, 1985.

Myers, L. M. and Richard L. Hoffman. *The Roots of Modern English*, Second Edition, University of Oklahoma Press, 1980.

Norgate, G. LE Grys. *The Life of Sir Walter Scott*, Methuen & CO., 1906.

Nuttall, P. Austin. *Johnson's Dictionary of the English Language, for the Use of Schools and General Students*. G. Routledge & Co., 1855.

Ousby, Ian. *Literary Britain and Ireland*, A & C Black, 1990.

Pearson, Hesketh. *Walter Scott: His Life and Personality*, Methuen & CO. Ltd., 1954.

Price, Mary R. *A Portrait of Britain 1066-1485*, Oxford University Press, 1987.

Price, Mary R. and C. E. L. Mather. *A Portrait of Britain 1485-1688*, Oxford University

Press, 1988.

Reed, James. *Sir Walter Scott: Landscape and Locality*, The Athlone Press, 1980.

Reeves, Lorna. *Tea & Sweets ; Fabulous Desserts for Afternoon Tea*, Hoffman Media, 2014.

Russell, Bertrand. *History of Western Philosophy*, Routledge Classics, 1996.

Sancha, Sheila. *The Castle Story*, Collins, 1991.

Shaw, Harry E. *Critical Essays on Sir Walter Scott: The Waverley Novels*, G. K. Hall & Co., 1996.

Sutherland, John. *The Life of Walter Scott*, Blackwell Publishers, 1995.

Steves, Rick and Gene Openshaw. *Rick Steves London*, Avalon Travel Hachette Book Group, 2023.

Till, Antonia. *The Collected Poems of William Wordsworth*, Wordsworth Poetry Library, 2006.

Thornley, G.C. and Gwyneth Roberts. *An Outline of English Literature*, Longman, 1993.

Vansittart, Peter. *London: A Literary Companion*, John Murray, 1994.

Vendler, Helen. *The Art of Shakespeare's Sonnets*, The Belknap Press of Harvard University Press, 1997.

Warburton, Nigel. *A Little History of Philosophy*, Yale University Press, 2011.

Watson, Bruce. *Old London Bridge: Lost and Found*, Museum of London, 2004.

Wilson, A. N. *A Life of Walter Scott*, Mandarin, 1996.

Wittich, John. *London Villages*, Shire Publications Ltd, 1992.

Wood, John Cunningham. *Karl Marx's Economics: Critical Assessments Volume I, II*, Croom Helm, 1988.

出口保夫『ロンドン・ブリッジ聖なる橋の2000年』朝日イブニングニュース社 1984.
―――『ロンドン漱石文学散歩』旺文社 1986.
―――『漱石のロンドン風景』（共編著）中公文庫 1995.
―――『漱石とともにロンドンを歩く』ランダムハウス講談社 2007.
―――『物語・大英博物館』中公新書 2005.

西野博道『イギリスの古城を旅する』双葉社 1995，双葉文庫 2000.
―――『戦略戦術兵器事典 5　ヨーロッパ城郭編』（共著）学習研究社 1997.
―――「イギリスの城と城郭都市」（出口保夫他編『21世紀イギリス文化を知る事典』）東京書籍 2009.
―――*The Future of English Spreading Around the World; A Brief History of English Language and Literature*, 流通経済大学出版会 2023.

AFTERWORD

On May 6, 2023, Charles III (1948-) and Camilla (1947-) were crowned as King and Queen of England respectively, at Westminster Abbey in London. Just one week later, Yasumasa, my second born son, arrived in London. If I remember, just one year before his going to Britain, my son dropped out of high school due to some circumstances, and transferred to a correspondence high school. But even after that, his depressed feelings did not improve. Then he often hung around all day long not to concentrate on anything. Considering he was very stressed out and had so much free time, the two of us consulted each other and he decided to go to London to study English for a short period of time. Then he went to England alone. However, on his third day in London, he contacted me and said over the phone, "Daddy, I regret coming to London." He felt it wasn't what he thought. The atmosphere of the homestay and the state of the language school were all different from what he had expected. He couldn't adapt well with them. After listening to his story, I told him that he didn't have to go to a language school anymore. Instead, I asked him to take pictures of London every day because he was going to stay in London for more than a month. Since then, he began to take a large number of pictures and dutifully sent them to my mobile phone, no matter what kind of photo it was. Early in the morning, as I opened my mobile and looked at many interesting photos, I really wanted to add a description or explanation of each photo. Then I decided to make something like a private photo book to present to him after he returned to Japan. As I continued to work, I gradually wanted to make a London guidebook for tourists. However, as I wrote a comment about each of the exciting pictures, such as, Big Ben, London Eye, Tower Bridge, etc., the sentence gradually became longer and longer, and the content became voluminous. Dealing with British culture, history, and literature, the contents were different from the original purpose. It seems to have turned out to be an essay book dealing with a theory of Britain such as "What is Britishness?", or "What is the essence of being British?" It was an eternal theme that I had held in my mind for a long time. Then, the endless topics were narrowed down considerably, limiting them to about 15 themes. The aim was to create a book that could be used as a textbook in several of my classes at universities. I also hoped for people who like Britain to read it and learn about Britain in a little more depth, or for people who are involved in English education to enjoy reading this book. That's how this book came to be.

As for the part about Shakespeare, originally, some of the contents were revised and added from the paper 'Blooming English in Shakespeare's Time' submitted to Tokyo Future University Bulletin 2023 Vol.17. Incidentally, Marx's article is from the paper 'A Study of the Future Vision of Philosophy – From the Perspective of the History of Western Philosophy –' submitted to Ryutsu Keizai Daigaku Ronshu (The Journal of Ryutsu Keizai University), Vol. 57, No.3.

View of the City from Alexandra Park

January, 2023, with corrections added. The descriptions of Chaucer, Charlotte Brontë, Conan Doyle, Wordsworth, and others also overlap somewhat with those covered in *The Future of English Spreading Around the World*, which was published last year in April 2023, regarding the history of the English language and the history of English literature. Of course, all of them have been added and modified to further develop the content. In addition, I think there are many contents in this book that overlap with what I have spoken at cultural lectures that I have given to the general public in various places, what I have lectured at many universities, and what I have written in books and magazines. In a way, this book is a compilation of my long-standing involvement with Britain.

As I mentioned at the beginning, most of the photographs used in this book (over 100 photos) were taken by my second son. In addition, some of the photos were provided by me, the author of this book (p.9, pp.40-41, p.68, pp.79-80, p.113, p.139, p.149 left, p.150 above, p.151, p.155). Others are from the public domain, mainly portraits (pp.10-11, pp.22-23, p.25, p.34, pp.38-39, p.44, p.47, p.54, pp.57-58, p.63, p.77, p.81 below, p.82 below, p.83, pp.89-90, pp.98-99, p.104, p.110, pp.118-119, p.125, p.127 right, p.128, p.130, p.148, p.149 right).

I would like to take this opportunity to thank all the staff involved in the production of this book for their cooperation. Finally, again, I would like to thank Mr. Ei Onozaki of Ryutsu Keizai University Press.

Hiromichi Nishino

THE AUTHOR

西野　博道（にしの・ひろみち）

東京都出身。早稲田大学卒業、同専攻科修了、同大学院修士課程修了。専攻は英語英文学。現在、東京理科大学、東京未来大学、文教大学、茨城大学、流通経済大学ほか非常勤講師。著書に『イギリスの古城を旅する』（双葉社）『戦略戦術兵器事典⑤ヨーロッパ城郭編』（共著・学習研究社）『美神を追いて－イギリス・ロマン派の系譜』（共著・音羽書房鶴見書店）『21世紀イギリス文化を知る事典』（共著・東京書籍）『スコットランド文化事典』（共著・原書房）*The Future of English Spreading Around the World*（流通経済大学出版会）のほか『埼玉の城址30選』（埼玉新聞社）『江戸城の縄張りをめぐる』（幹書房）『関東の城址を歩く』『英傑を生んだ日本の城址を歩く』（さきたま出版会）『日本の城郭－築城者の野望』『日本の城郭－名将のプライド』（柏書房）など日英城郭研究の成果を踏まえた著書が多数ある。'The History of Japanese Castles with the Perspective of British Castles'（流通經濟大學論集 2021.10）'A Study of the Future Vision of Philosophy — From the Perspective of the History of Western Philosophy'（流通經濟大學論集 2023.1）等はネット公開されているので是非ご覧ください。

PHOTOGRAPHY

西野　康真（にしの・やすまさ）

2005年愛媛県西条市生まれ。趣味はロック（ストリートダンス）、ピアノ・ギター演奏、作詞作曲。14歳で英検2級、16歳で英検準1級合格。その後、英国留学を希望するがCovid-19の世界蔓延によって渡英を断念。2023年5月、単身で渡英しロンドンの語学学校に入学する。

バッキンガム宮殿にて

Discovering London in the 21st Century

発行日　2024年 3 月 1 日　初版発行

著　者　西　野　博　道

発行者　上　野　裕　一

発行所　流通経済大学出版会
　　　　〒301-8555　茨城県龍ヶ崎市120
　　　　電話　0297-60-1167　FAX　0297-60-1165

ⒸHiromichi Nishino, 2024
Printed in Japan/アベル社
ISBN978-4-911205-02-0 C0098 ¥1800E